USBORNE
FACTS & FUN
ABOUT
GEOGRAPHY AND HISTORY

USBORNE
FACTS & FUN
ABOUT
GEOGRAPHY AND HISTORY

SCHOLASTIC INC.
New York Toronto London Auckland Sydney

ISBN 0-590-62143-2

Geography Quizbook copyright © 1992 by Usborne Publishing Ltd. First published in Great Britain in 1992 by Usborne Publishing Ltd. History Quizbook copyright © 1991 by Usborne Publishing Ltd. First published in Great Britain in 1991 by Usborne Publishing Ltd. All rights reserved. Published by Scholastic Inc., 555 Broadway, New York, NY 10012, by arrangement with Usborne Publishing Ltd.

12 11 10 9 8 7 6 5 4 3 2   8 9/9 0 1/0

Printed in the U.S.A.   08

First Scholastic printing, January 1996

Contents

USBORNE
FACTS & FUN
ABOUT
GEOGRAPHY AND HISTORY

Part One
USBORNE FACTS & FUN ABOUT GEOGRAPHY

Marit Claridge and Paul Dowswell

Edited by Judy Tatchell

Designed by Ruth Russell

Illustrated by Chris Lyon

Additional design and illustration by
Richard Johnson and Rachel Lockwood

Consultant: John Brennan

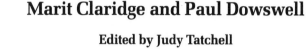

Contents

About Part One

The earth's surface is immensely varied. Part One of the book looks at our planet, from mountains to rainforests, oceans to cities. It explains how the planet provides its inhabitants with air, water and food, and shows why we need to protect the earth from the growing threat of pollution.

How to do the quizzes

Throughout the book there are quiz questions to answer as you go along, printed in italic type, *like this*. Some of the questions rely on your general knowledge, others have clues elsewhere on the page. Keep a note of your answers and check them against the answers on pages 28-31.

The Geography Megaquiz

On pages 26-27 is the Geography Megaquiz - a set of ten quick quizzes to test you on your general knowledge and what you have read about in Part One.

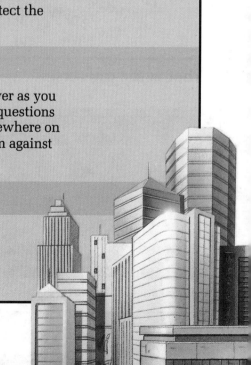

The Earth in space

Planet Earth is a huge ball of rock which spins in space. Earth is one of the smallest of nine planets which circle around a central star, called the Sun. A group of planets circling around a star is called a solar system.

What is a star?

A star is a burning ball of gas which gives off heat and light. The Sun is a star. It is part of a group of millions of stars, called a galaxy. There are about 200,000 million stars in our galaxy which is called the Milky Way. Many stars are bigger than the Sun.

1. A solar system is made up of a star and: a) a sun; b) a galaxy; c) planets.

The Milky Way

Sun

Mercury

Venus

Moon

Earth

The furthest that anyone has ever travelled is to the Moon. The first men landed on the Moon on 20 July 1969.

4. Is the Moon a star?

5. The first man on the moon was: a) Christopher Columbus; b) Neil Armstrong; c) Flash Gordon.

6. Which is the coldest planet?

Mars

Jupiter

One of Jupiter's 12 moons. A moon circles around a planet, not around the Sun.

Asteroids – rocks circling the Sun.

7. Which planet is named after the Roman goddess of love?

8. Which is bigger, a solar system or the Milky Way?

9. Unscramble these words to find the names of two planets: I STAR JUMPER.

Uranus

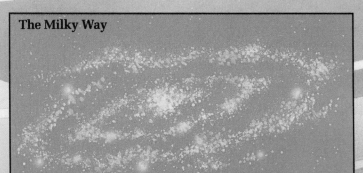

Your address in space would look like this:

Name
House
Street
Town
Country
The Earth
The Solar System
The Milky Way
The Universe

What is the universe?

Four galaxies in the universe.

Our galaxy, the Milky Way, is part of a group of about thirty galaxies. Beyond this there may be more than 200,000 million other galaxies. Together they make up the universe. No one knows how big the universe is.

2. Is the earth the center of the universe?

3. Distances between stars are measured in: a) light years; b) string; c) gallons.

Why does it get dark at night?

The earth spins around all the time. It takes about 24 hours to spin around once. As it spins, some parts of it face away from the sun and are in shadow (nighttime) and some parts have sunlight (daytime).

day.

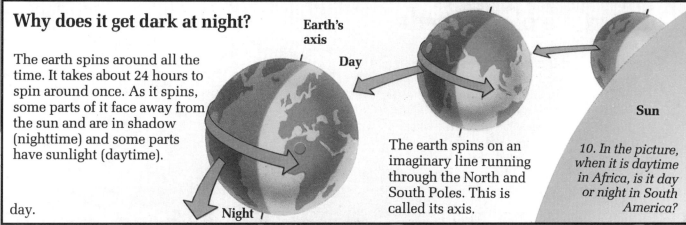

Earth's axis

Day

Sun

The earth spins on an imaginary line running through the North and South Poles. This is called its axis.

Night

10. In the picture, when it is daytime in Africa, is it day or night in South America?

Why do the hours of daylight differ?

In most parts of the world the hours of daylight gradually increase and then shorten as the year goes by. This happens because the earth is tilted on its axis as it travels around the sun. Depending on the time of year, either the north or the south has longer hours of daylight.

Between April and September the northern part of the world tilts towards the sun. Countries here spend more hours in daylight as the earth goes through its 24-hour spin.

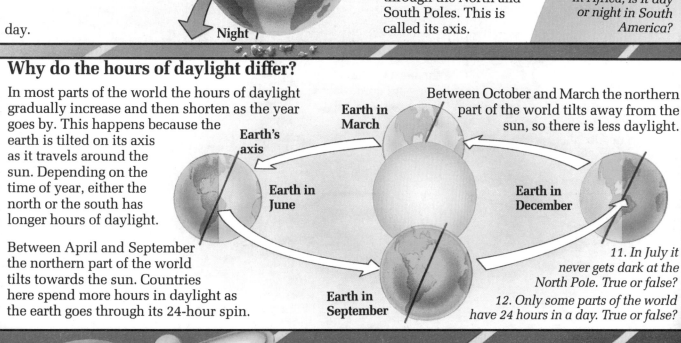

Earth's axis

Earth in March

Earth in June

Between October and March the northern part of the world tilts away from the sun, so there is less daylight.

Earth in December

Earth in September

11. In July it never gets dark at the North Pole. True or false?

12. Only some parts of the world have 24 hours in a day. True or false?

Saturn

Saturn's rings – these are made of millions of ice-covered rocks.

One of Saturn's moons.

Did you know?

The earth circles the sun at a speed of 18.5 miles (29.8km) per second. It takes 365¼ days to make one complete circle around the sun.

We use the 365 days to measure one year. Every fourth year the extra quarters are added together to make a year with 366 days, which is called a leap year.

13. Do all planets have moons?

14. Is there life on Neptune?

Why does the moon change shape?

The half of the moon facing the sun is always lit up. As the moon goes around the earth, you see different parts of this half. The moon takes about a month to go around the earth.

The bottom part of the picture shows the moon in five positions, which it passes through on its way around the earth. The pink band shows what the moon looks like from the earth.

Neptune

15. Is a New Moon visible?

Pluto

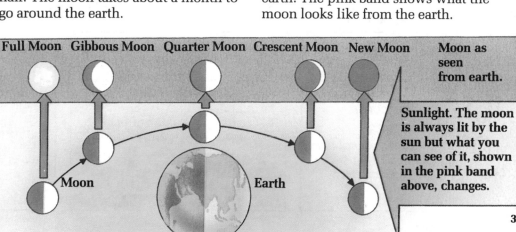

Full Moon Gibbous Moon Quarter Moon Crescent Moon New Moon Moon as seen from earth.

Moon

Earth

Sunlight. The moon is always lit by the sun but what you can see of it, shown in the pink band above, changes.

3

The surface of the earth

If you could look at the earth from space, you would see a brownish-green, blue and white planet, half hidden in swirling clouds. The blue oceans make up 71% of the surface of the earth. The brownish-green areas are the land, which is in seven main blocks, called continents.

People live on about a third of the land on earth. Some parts are crowded. Others, such as deserts, are nearly empty.

1. Seen from space, what color would the Arctic and Antarctic be?

2. Which is the largest continent?

The areas around the North and South Poles are frozen all the time. The North Pole is in the middle of the Arctic Ocean.

3. Do people live at the North Pole?

Mountains cover nearly a quarter of the land on earth. They are cold places and few people live there.

4. Mountains make good farmland. True or false?

Arctic Ocean

5. In which continent are the Himalayas?

Europe

Asia

North America

Pacific Ocean

The Pacific Ocean is the largest ocean. It covers nearly one third of the surface of the earth.

Atlantic Ocean

Africa

Indian Ocean

Australia

South America

The South Pole is in the continent of Antarctica.

6. Are there more people or penguins in Antarctica?

There are volcanoes, valleys, plains and mountains on the ocean floor, just as there are on land.

Southern Ocean

Antarctica

Deserts have almost no water. The Sahara is the largest desert in the world.

7. The Sahara covers almost one third of Africa. True or false?

Most people live on flat land in places that are neither too hot nor too cold. Many people live along rivers where there is rich farmland.

8. The River Nile flows through: a) Ecuador; b) Egypt; c) England.

Very few people live in the hot, wet rainforests around the middle of the Earth.

9. Brazil has the largest rainforest. True or false?

4

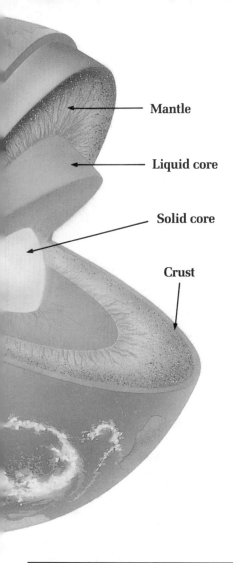

Mantle

Liquid core

Solid core

Crust

Is the earth solid?

The earth is made up of layers. The continents and oceans are part of an outer layer of solid rock called the crust. This rests on hot, toffee-like rock called the mantle.

The center of the earth, the core, is made of very hot, heavy rock. Scientists think that the core is liquid on the outside and solid in the middle.

Do the continents move?

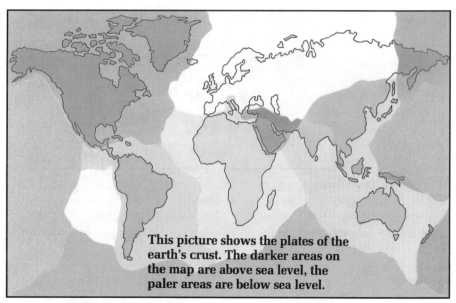

This picture shows the plates of the earth's crust. The darker areas on the map are above sea level, the paler areas are below sea level.

The continents are part of the earth's crust, which is made up of several huge pieces, like a big jigsaw puzzle. These pieces, or plates, are shown on the map. The mantle underneath the crust is heated by the liquid rocks around the earth's core. This sets up currents in the mantle, in the same way that boiling water swirls

around in a saucepan. These currents move some of the plates together while other plates move apart. The main mountain ranges, volcanoes and earthquake zones all run along the edges of the plates

10. Is is hotter at the center of the earth or in the Sahara desert?

11. Africa was once joined to America. True or false?

Did you know?

The earth's crust is about 40 miles (64km) thick. If the earth was the size of a soccer ball, the crust would be the thickness of a postage stamp.

What happens when the earth's crust moves?

When plates move together, the crust is slowly pushed up into folds. These are mountains. The highest mountains in the world, the Himalayas, were formed when India bumped into Asia.

12. The lowest places on earth are at the bottom of: a) the sea; b) lakes; c) mineshafts.

Pressure builds up as plates push or slide against each other. If the pressure becomes too great, the rocks suddenly snap and move, shaking the ground. This is called an earthquake.

13. Which of these cities is famous for its earthquakes: a) Paris; b) San Francisco; c) Sydney?

Volcanoes occur along the edges of plates as these are the weakest spots in the earth's crust. The hot, liquid rock under the crust forces its way through the surface as a volcano.

14. Can volcanoes erupt under the sea?

15. What is the name of the world's highest mountain?

Volcano

Plates pressing together. ⟶

Folds of rock

Mapping the world

A map is a picture of any part of the earth. A map can be of a very small area, such as a museum, or of a whole country, a continent or the whole world.

Maps can show different things, such as roads or what sort of food is grown in an area. They help you to find out where places are on the earth and how to get there.

How are flat maps made of the earth?

It is difficult to draw a flat map of the earth because the earth is ball-shaped. The picture above shows how a mapmaker might draw a map of a ball. The ball is divided into segments which are then spread out flat. Parts of the ball have to be stretched on the map to fill the gaps between the segments.

In the same way, mapmakers have to change the shape of countries slightly to make flat maps of the earth. There are several ways of stretching out a ball-shape to fit on a flat surface. These are called projections. The maps above show how two different projections make

Australia appear to be two different shapes.

1. Which is more accurate, a globe or a flat map?

2. Which continent is missing from this list: Australia, Europe, Africa, North America, Antarctica, South America?

What is a political map?

A political map shows how the earth is divided up into countries. A country is an area that is usually run by its own government. This political map shows the countries in South America.

3. Would you use a political map to find a country's borders, or to find where mountains are?

4. How many countries are there in South America?

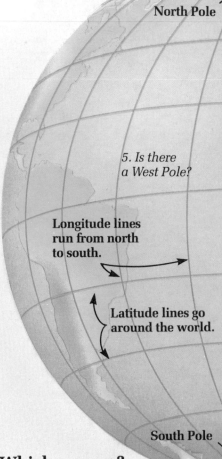

North Pole

5. Is there a West Pole?

Longitude lines run from north to south.

Latitude lines go around the world.

South Pole

Which way up?

The four main directions used on maps are north, south, east and west.

North is the direction towards the North Pole from anywhere on Earth. South is the direction towards the South Pole. When you face north, the direction to your left is west and to your right is east. North is normally at the top of a map.

6. What is the direction half way between north and east?

How do you find North?

You can use a compass to find out which way you are facing. The needle of a compass always points north.

Turn the compass until the needle points to letter N. You can then see which way is west, east or south.

7. Which direction is at the bottom of most maps?

Longitude 0° runs through Greenwich in England.

Latitude 0° is called the **Equator**. It is half way between the North and South Poles.

8. Can space travellers see latitude and longitude lines on the earth?

9. Greenwich is in: a) Madrid; b) Paris; c) London.

Why are there lines on a map?

Lines are drawn on maps to divide them into sections. The lines help you to find places on a map. On continental and world maps, the distances between the lines are measured in degrees (°).

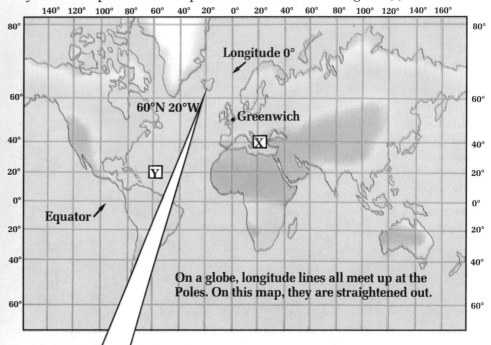

Longitude 0°

60°N 20°W

Greenwich

X

Y

Equator

On a globe, longitude lines all meet up at the Poles. On this map, they are straightened out.

Did you know?

You can use the stars to find your direction. In the northern half of the world (called the northern hemisphere), look for a group of stars called the Big Dipper. A line through the end of the Dipper points to the North Star. This is directly above the North Pole.

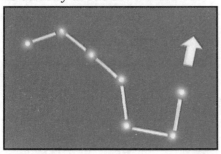

In the southern hemisphere, look for the Southern Cross to find which way is south.

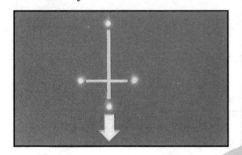

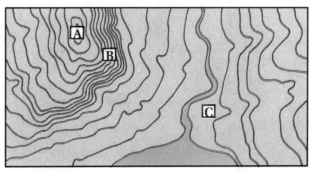

Imagine two ships colliding at sea. They radio for help and tell the rescue services that their position is 60°N and 20°W. This means 60° north of the Equator and 20° west of longitude 0° (the north-south line running through Greenwich). The rescue service can pinpoint their position at once and direct any nearby ship to their aid.

10. Are the ships nearer North America or Europe?

11. If a volcano erupted at point X on the map, what would its position be?

12. If a hurricane was approaching Central America from point Y, what would its position be?

What is a physical map?

A physical map shows the earth's natural features – such as rivers, mountains and valleys. Lines on some maps, called contour lines, indicate the height of the land in regular intervals. The closer together these lines are, the steeper the slope. This map shows the coastline at the bottom of the page.

A

B

C

13. Is there flat land on the map at A, B or C?

14. Is it very steep at A, B or C?

15. Is A, B or C at the top of a hill?

The earth's atmosphere

The earth is wrapped in a layer of air, called the atmosphere. The air acts like a blanket around the earth. During the day it protects the earth from the sun's harmful rays. At night it stops heat from leaving the earth.

Air is a mixture of gases. The main gas is nitrogen. Most of the rest, about 20% of air, is oxygen.

1. Which gas do you need to breathe in order to stay alive?

How high is the sky?

The earth's atmosphere is about 20 miles (32km) thick. Beyond this is space and the other planets and stars in the universe. The picture below shows what happens at different levels of the atmosphere.

20 miles (32km) **Scientists send research balloons up to 18 miles (30km) high.**

11 miles (18km) **There may be clouds in the sky up to here.**

10 miles (16km) **The weather affects the atmosphere up to about this level.**

9.3 miles (15km) **Jets cruise at about this level.**

5.5 miles (8.8km) **Mount Everest**

2. Are jets affected by storms?

3. At 0 miles (0km) it is: a) ground level; b) sea level; c) sky level.

Did you know?

Although you cannot feel the air around you, it does have a weight. Altogether the air in the earth's atmosphere weighs about 5,000 million tons (tonnes). The weight of air is called air pressure.

4. Air pressure is less at the top of a mountain than at sea level. True or false?

What causes the wind?

The air around the earth is always moving. You feel this moving air as wind.

At the Equator the land heats the air. Warm air is lighter than cold air so it rises. Warm air rising makes an area of low air pressure. Cold air is sucked in from elsewhere to take the place of the warm air.

At the Poles, air presses down on the earth and makes an area of high air pressure. The wind is caused by air moving from areas of high pressure to low pressure areas.

5. Is it hot or cold at the Equator?

6. Which of these tells which way the wind is blowing: a) weather vane; b) compass; c) barometer?

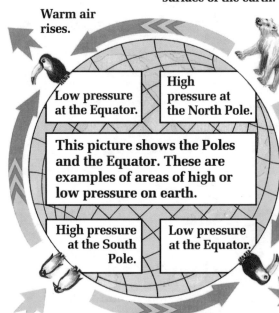

Cold air presses heavily on the surface of the earth.

Warm air rises.

Low pressure at the Equator.

High pressure at the North Pole.

This picture shows the Poles and the Equator. These are examples of areas of high or low pressure on earth.

High pressure at the South Pole.

Low pressure at the Equator.

Cold air, as wind, flows to take the place of rising warm air.

What are weather and climate?

Weather is sunshine, wind, rain, snow and so on. In some parts of the world, the weather is much the same day after day. In other places, the weather changes all the time.

A place's climate is the average amount of sunshine, wind and rainfall that it has, year after year.

7. It is warmer on a mountain top, which is nearer the sun, than at sea level. True or false?

You see rainbows when sunlight shines through raindrops.

Snowflakes are made of tiny ice crystals. Each one is different.

8. Which has more changeable weather, the Sahara desert or Great Britain?

9. Are weather and climate the same thing?

What are clouds?

Clouds are patches of air which contain millions of tiny drops of water. Clouds have different shapes and are at different heights. Some are shown below.

Cirrus clouds are very high and are made of tiny ice crystals. They usually mean rain is coming.

Cirrocumulus clouds are a sign of unsettled weather.

Cumulonimbus clouds often bring thunderstorms with rain, snow or hail.

Cumulus clouds appear in sunny, summer skies.

Stratus cloud is a low blanket of cloud which often brings drizzle.

Fog is cloud at ground level.

10. Which are the highest clouds in the sky?

11. Smog is a mixture of smoke and: a) rain; b) smelly dog; c) fog.

What are thunder and lightning?

Lightning makes the air it goes through very hot. The air expands violently, like an explosion, and makes a clap of thunder. Below, you can see what causes lightning.

Inside cumulonimbus clouds, particles of water and ice move up and down in air currents.
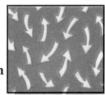

As the water and ice rub against each other, there is a build-up of static electricity.

The electricity builds up until there is a giant spark. You see this as a flash of lightning.

You can tell how far away a thunderstorm is by counting the time between the lightning and the first clap of thunder. The distance is about a mile (about 2km) for every five seconds.

12. If you hear thunder ten seconds after seeing lightning, how far away is the storm?

13. Are there more thunderstorms at the Equator or at the Poles?

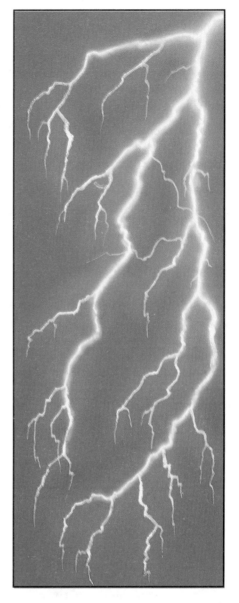

What are hurricanes and tornadoes?

A hurricane is a violent storm with strong winds and rain. Areas of extremely low pressure build up over warm oceans. Warm, wet air spins into the middle of the low pressure area causing the strong winds. The warm air rises and the water vapor in it becomes clouds and heavy rain.

14. Hurricanes have eyes. True or false?

A tornado is like a very small hurricane. It is a whirling funnel of upward-spinning air. Winds in a tornado reach up to 300mph (500kmph). They suck up anything in their path, sometimes even people, animals and cars.

15. Tornadoes can pick up trains. True or false?

Rivers and rain

Plants and animals need water to stay alive. Your body is about 75% water. Without water, your body would not work.

Only 3% of the water on earth is fresh water. The rest is salty. Two thirds of the earth's fresh water is frozen in ice sheets and glaciers. The remaining third is in rivers, lakes and water underground.

1. Camels can survive without water for: a) 21; b) 7; c) 2 days.

Where does water come from?

There is always the same amount of water on earth. It moves from place to place. When a puddle dries up, the water does not disappear. Tiny particles of water rise from the puddle. They become a gas called water vapor. This is called evaporation.

When water vapor rises into cooler air, it turns back into tiny water droplets and becomes clouds and rain. The movement of water from the land to the air and back to the land is called the water cycle.

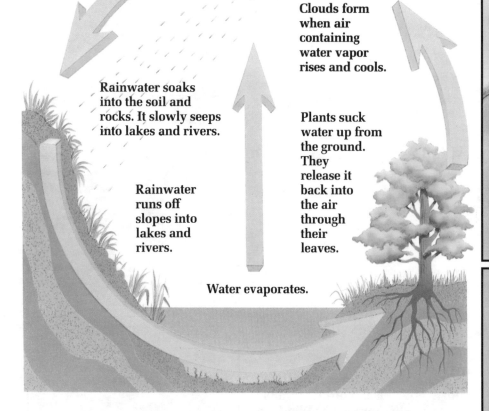

Clouds form when air containing water vapor rises and cools.

Rainwater soaks into the soil and rocks. It slowly seeps into lakes and rivers.

Plants suck water up from the ground. They release it back into the air through their leaves.

Rainwater runs off slopes into lakes and rivers.

Water evaporates.

2. When washing dries, the water in it: a) disappears; b) becomes water vapor; c) becomes air.

3. What are clouds made of?

4. In big cities, each glass of water someone drinks has already been drunk by someone else. True or false?

5. Is there water vapor in your breath?

Where do rivers begin?

Rivers begin in hills and mountains as small streams. They carry rainwater from the land to the sea. A river gets bigger as it collects more and more water on its way.

6. Which of these rivers is the shortest: a) Thames; b) Nile; c) Amazon?

As the water flows downhill it sweeps away small pieces of rock. These rub at the bottom and sides of the stream and make it wider and deeper.

Rivers flood when there is more rain than usual on the land which drains into the river.

7. Some rivers flow uphill. True or false?

Did you know?

You need to drink about 3 pints (1.7 liters) of water a day. Where there is plenty of water, each person uses about 20 times as much as this a day, for washing, cooking and so on.

8. What happens to water at 32°F (0°C)?

9. You can live without water for: a) a day; b) four days; c) a month.

What is hydroelectricity?

The power in falling water can be used to make electricity, which is then called hydroelectricity. The water is trapped by a dam. It is then piped to a power station where it flows over big water wheels, called turbines. These turn generators which make electricity.

River water also has enormous power. It wears away rocks and shapes the land into hills and valleys.

10. Hydroelectric power stations are only found in flat areas. True or false?

11. What do hydroelectric, tidal and wave power have in common?

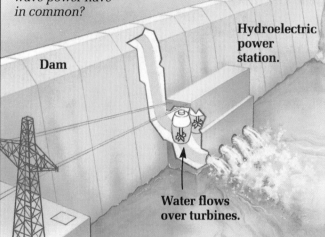

Dam

Hydroelectric power station.

Water flows over turbines.

How is a waterfall made?

When a river flows from hard to softer rock, the softer rock wears away more quickly and makes a small step. The water falls over the step on to the soft rock below, wearing it away even more. Gradually the step and the waterfall get bigger.

Hard rock   **Soft rock**

Waterfall

The highest waterfall in the world is Angel Falls in Venezuela. The river drops 3,214ft (979m).

12. Which of these is not a famous waterfall: a) Niagara; b) Grand Canyon; c) Victoria?

What is water pollution?

Many towns and factories are built near rivers so that they can use the water. Sometimes towns and factories pour dirty water back into the rivers. The rivers become dirty, or "polluted." Pollution can make rivers smell and can kill water plants and animals. Polluted rivers drain into the sea and pollute the sea as well. (See pages 24-25 for more about pollution.)

13. Fish caught in polluted rivers can be poisonous. True or false?

Farmers spray chemicals on fields to make crops grow better. The chemicals may drain into streams and rivers and pollute them.

People sometimes dump rubbish in rivers. As rubbish rots, it uses up oxygen in the water. Fish may die due to lack of oxygen.

Some harmful cleaning chemicals in waste water from homes remain harmful even after treatment in a sewage treatment plant.

Rubbish from towns is often buried in huge holes in the ground. Chemicals in rubbish can drain through the ground into rivers.

What is a glacier?

Glaciers are rivers of ice. They occur in very cold areas and on high mountains. When snow falls here it crushes snow beneath it to ice. The snow and ice slide slowly down the mountain.

14. Glaciers are found in: a) Mexico; b) Great Britain; c) Scandinavia.

Glacier

U-shaped valley

Glaciers wear away the sides and bottoms of valleys. They leave behind deep U-shaped valleys.

15. Which flows faster, a river or a glacier?

Oceans and coasts

Nearly three quarters of the earth's surface is covered by oceans. There are five oceans (see page 4) and they contain smaller areas called seas. The coast is where the land meets the sea.

The shape of the coasts is always changing. Waves pound at beaches and cliffs, slowly wearing them away. The sea also drops sand and mud in sheltered areas. This builds up and becomes new land.

1. Are all the oceans joined together?

2. Which of these is a sea, not an ocean: a) Atlantic; b) Pacific; c) Mediterranean; d) Indian?

Why is the sea salty?

Water dissolves salt in rocks on the ocean floor. On land, streams and rivers carry salt from rocks to the sea. Also, water evaporates from the sea leaving the salt behind.

River water does not taste salty because a river is continually filled with fresh water from rain or thawing snow. There is only a small amount of salt in it at any one time.

3. Can salt be collected from the sea?

4. There is gold in seawater. True or false?

How are cliffs formed?

Cliffs are formed where a hard band of rock meets the sea. Waves carrying small pebbles break against the rock just above sea level. They erode, or eat into it, and a small cliff is made. The sea continues to eat away at the rock and makes an overhang. In time the overhang breaks off, leaving a bigger cliff for the sea to beat against.

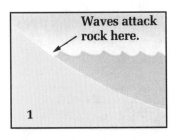

Waves attack rock here.

1

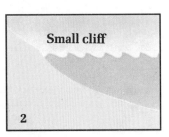

Small cliff

2

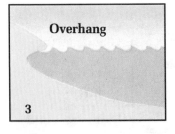

Overhang

3

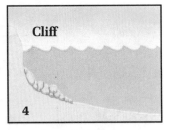

Cliff

4

5. Cliffs can form overnight. True or false?

6. Cliffs are only found on the coast. True or false?

How are beaches made?

Waves wash sand along the coast. When they reach a sheltered area they slow down, and drop the sand. In time, the sand builds up into beaches. Beaches are often found in sheltered bays.

Beach

Bay

Waves pound hardest on the headlands. Over many years the headlands are worn back and the coastline becomes smoother.

Headland

7. Which bird is not a seabird: a) starling; b) puffin; c) gannet?

The sea sometimes drops sand in the shelter of a headland. This makes a ridge of sand, called a spit.

Headland

Bay

Spit

What is sand?

Sand is tiny particles of rock. It is washed into the sea by rivers and made when waves grind down rocky cliffs. Sand is also made from broken down shells, and coral which is washed ashore from nearby reefs. Few plants can grow in the sand on the beach, but many tiny creatures live in it.

8. Do you find sand dunes on beaches or on cliff tops?

Did you know?

The icebergs that float in the oceans of the far north and far south of the world come from glaciers (see page 11). Some glaciers flow down from mountans into the sea, and huge chunks of ice break off them and float away. Icebergs also break off from the thick sheet of ice that covers most of Antarctica. Frozen water does not contain salt, so all icebergs are made up of fresh water.

9. How much of an iceberg can you see above water: a) one half; b) one quarter; c) one eighth?

10. Which famous British cruise liner was sunk on its first voyage in 1912, by an iceberg in the Atlantic?

How do people use the sea?

The picture below shows how people use the oceans and coasts for energy, transport, food and pleasure. Careless use of the sea has damaged this environment, though. Look for the red boxes which describe some of the ways in which people have polluted the sea.

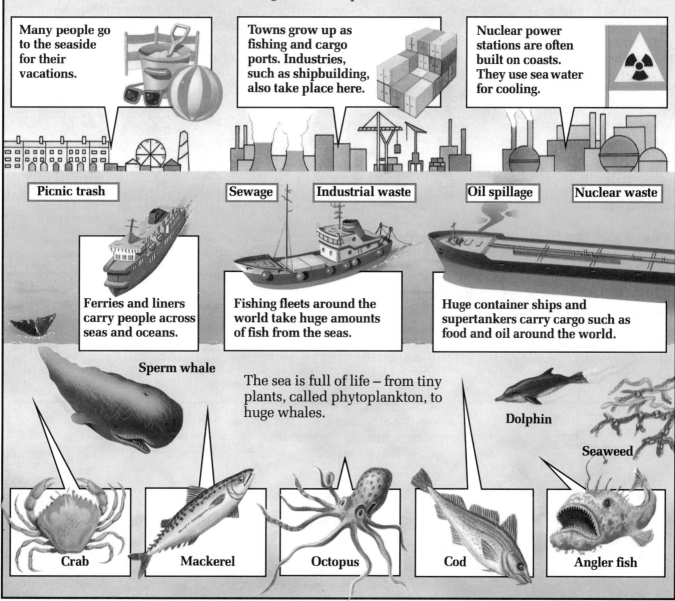

Many people go to the seaside for their vacations.

Towns grow up as fishing and cargo ports. Industries, such as shipbuilding, also take place here.

Nuclear power stations are often built on coasts. They use sea water for cooling.

Picnic trash **Sewage** **Industrial waste** **Oil spillage** **Nuclear waste**

Ferries and liners carry people across seas and oceans.

Fishing fleets around the world take huge amounts of fish from the seas.

Huge container ships and supertankers carry cargo such as food and oil around the world.

Sperm whale

The sea is full of life – from tiny plants, called phytoplankton, to huge whales.

Dolphin

Seaweed

Crab   Mackerel   Octopus   Cod   Angler fish

11. If attacked, an octopus will try to escape: a) in a cloud of black ink; b) on roller-skates; c) in the sand.

12. Can you eat seaweed?

13. How many of the sea animals in the picture are fish?

14. Fish living 10,000ft (3,000m) down in dark ocean waters can switch on lights. True or false?

Why do fish need protection?

When too many fish are taken from the sea, fewer fish are available to breed and numbers drop rapidly. Some countries are trying to make international laws to control the numbers of fish caught and to make fishing methods less cruel. Many sea creatures die unnecessarily in nets used to trap other fish. Thousands of dolphins, for instance, have been killed in huge nets called purse seines, used to catch tuna fish.

15. Dolphins are small whales. True or false?

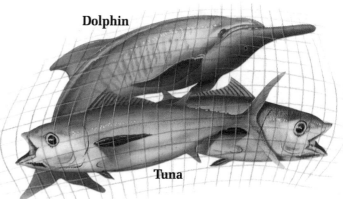

Dolphin

Tuna

People around the world

There are over 5,000 million people in the world. The world's population is now so large that there are more people alive today than have ever lived before. Most live where it is neither too hot nor too cold and there is a good supply of food.

Differences in skin color and face shape developed many thousands of years ago to help people to survive in one particular climate. For example, dark skin protected people in very hot countries from the sun. These differences are not so important today because modern clothes, houses and heating enable people of any physical type to live almost anywhere. Below are three of the most common types, or races, of people.

Negro people originally came from Africa.

1. Which race are Japanese people?

Caucasian people originally came from Europe and Asia.

Mongolian people originally came from Asia.

2. Which race are Scandinavian people?

Where did the first people come from?

People have not always lived all over the world. Scientists believe that the first people came from Africa. They could make tools to hunt with, and fire to keep themselves warm. When their numbers grew these skills enabled them to travel to cooler areas in search of fresh food supplies. The map below shows how people spread to the rest of the world from Africa.

3. The first humans might have hunted: a) camels; b) koalas; c) antelope.

4. No one lives in Antarctica because: a) there are only penguins to eat; b) it is too cold; c) the nightlife is dull.

5. One fifth of the world population today is Chinese. True or false?

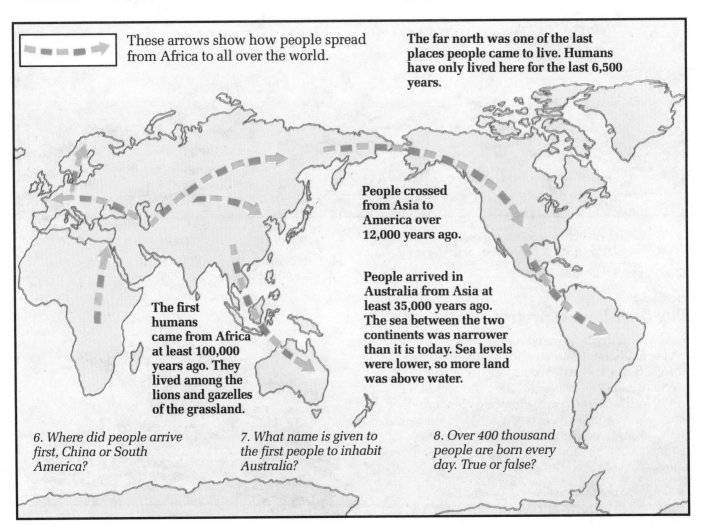

These arrows show how people spread from Africa to all over the world.

The far north was one of the last places people came to live. Humans have only lived here for the last 6,500 years.

People crossed from Asia to America over 12,000 years ago.

The first humans came from Africa at least 100,000 years ago. They lived among the lions and gazelles of the grassland.

People arrived in Australia from Asia at least 35,000 years ago. The sea between the two continents was narrower than it is today. Sea levels were lower, so more land was above water.

6. Where did people arrive first, China or South America?

7. What name is given to the first people to inhabit Australia?

8. Over 400 thousand people are born every day. True or false?

Why do people's lives vary so much?

People live very different lives across the world. Whether a country is rich or poor makes the greatest difference to the quality of everyday life. Religion, language and traditions also influence the way people live.

Families vary in size around the world. In rich countries like the USA, families have an average of two children. Many parents can afford to buy their children expensive clothes and possessions. Many children are encouraged to stay at school and are educated to a high standard.

9. Which of these items do not need electricity?

In poor countries like India, families usually have over six children. In some areas half these children die before they are five. Women have several children to make sure that some survive. Diseases carried in dirty water and sewage are the cause of most childhood deaths. Children cost their parents very little and by the age of 11 or 12 they can work and bring money into the home.

10. Throughout the world an average family has: a) one child; b) four children; c) ten children.

11. Which one of these is essential for any family: a) money; b) food and water; c) television; d) a home?

Did you know?

People in North America and Europe use about forty times as much energy, and eat three times as much food, as people in poor countries in Asia and Africa.

Which country has the most people?

China has the most people. There are over a thousand million Chinese. Two-thirds of them work on farms, which grow enough to feed this huge population. The government encourages couples to have only one child, to stop the population from getting so big it would be impossible to feed.

Rice is the main crop. It grows easily, but needs a lot of water.

A wide hat protects against the hot sun.

Almost all farming is done by hand, rather than with machinery.

12. Which one of these is not a Chinese dish: a) Chow mein; b) Dim sum; c) Shanghai?

How long do people live?

Throughout the world the average lifetime is around 64 years. People currently live the longest in Japan – the world's richest country. Men can expect to live to around 76 and women to around 82.

In Japan people eat a healthy diet. They eat more fish than any other country, and very little fat. Fish is often eaten raw, like this dish on the right, called *sushi.* Health services are good. Most people's lives are stable and comfortable.

Afghanistan is one country where people have much shorter lives. Few people live beyond forty. War, famine and disease are common and health services are poor.

Chopsticks

13. Which continent is Afghanistan in?

How many languages are there?

There are over 5,000 languages in daily use in the world. Mandarin is the most spoken one. It is used by two thirds of the Chinese population – 770 million people. Over 330 million people grow up speaking English, but around 1,000 million people learn it as an additional language. This pie chart represents all the people in the world. It shows how many speak Mandarin, and how many speak English as a first (dark blue) or second (light blue) language.

14. A mandarin is also a type of: a) lemon; b) orange; c) banana; d) grape.

15. The Romans spread the English language around the world. True or false?

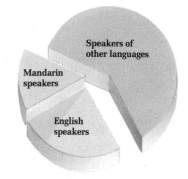

Speakers of other languages

Mandarin speakers

English speakers

Cities and towns

The first people on earth moved from place to place hunting animals and gathering wild fruits and seeds to eat. There were no villages, towns or cities.

About 10,000 years ago, people in some places began to keep animals and grow crops. This enabled them to stay and make homes in one place. These homes were the beginnings of villages, towns and cities. Today, about one third of the world's people live in towns and cities.

1. Which lived on earth first, dinosaurs or people?

2. Which of these cities was built first: a) Rome; b) Los Angeles; c) Hong Kong?

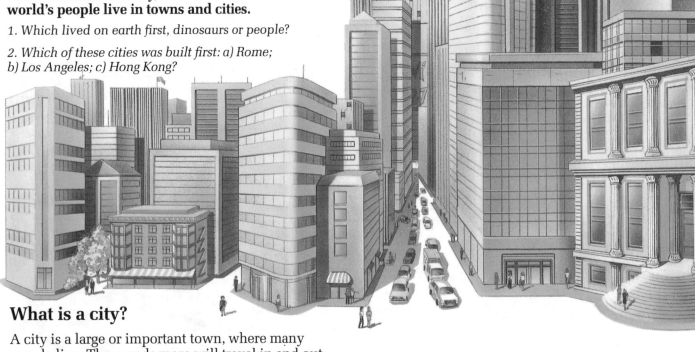

Tall buildings make the best use of land, which can be expensive in city centers.

What is a city?

A city is a large or important town, where many people live. Thousands more will travel in and out of a big city every day. Some come to work, others to shop or visit professional people such as hospital doctors. Cities are busy, bustling places and city roads are often jammed with traffic – especially when people are travelling to and from work or school. Here are some of the things you might find in a city.

3. Village people might need to visit a town or city to buy: a) bread; b) a newspaper; c) a compact disc.

4. Would cities be cleaner and quieter if everyone came into them on buses and trains, or in their own cars?

5. Put these forms of transport in order of their invention: motorbike, aircraft, train.

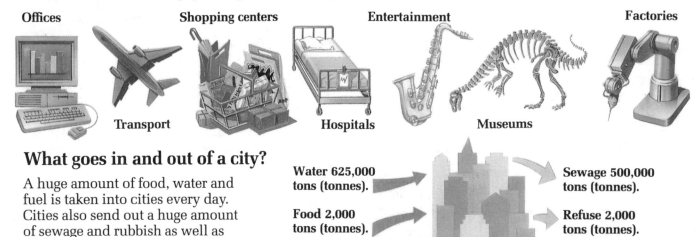

Offices · Shopping centers · Transport · Hospitals · Entertainment · Museums · Factories

What goes in and out of a city?

A huge amount of food, water and fuel is taken into cities every day. Cities also send out a huge amount of sewage and rubbish as well as dirt into the air. The picture on the right shows roughly how much goes into and out of an American city of about a million people each day.

Water 625,000 tons (tonnes).

Food 2,000 tons (tonnes).

Fuel for heating, cooking and cars 9,500 tons (tonnes).

Sewage 500,000 tons (tonnes).

Refuse 2,000 tons (tonnes).

Air pollutants 950 tons (tonnes).

6. Chicago has nearly three million people. How much food will it need every day.

7. Air pollution is mostly caused by sewage works. True or false?

Where are cities built?

There is always a good reason why a town or city grows up where it does. The picture below shows what some of these reasons might be.

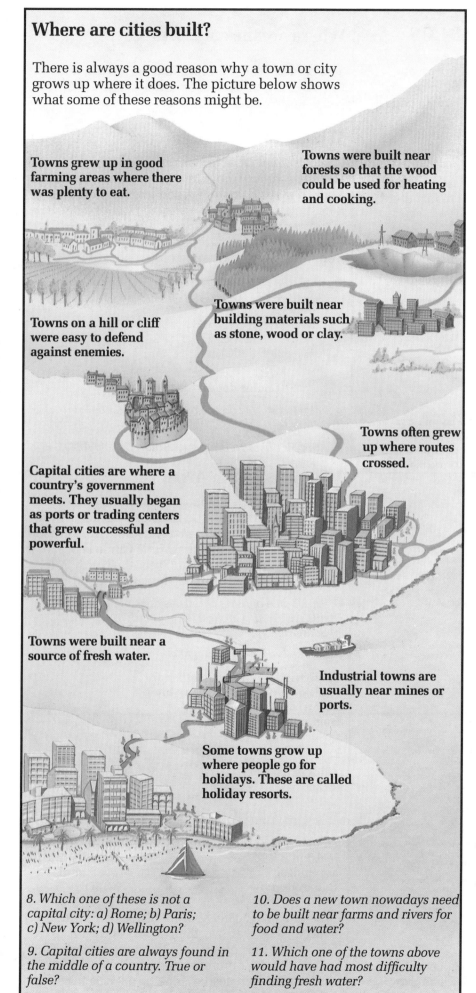

Towns grew up in good farming areas where there was plenty to eat.

Towns were built near forests so that the wood could be used for heating and cooking.

Towns on a hill or cliff were easy to defend against enemies.

Towns were built near building materials such as stone, wood or clay.

Towns often grew up where routes crossed.

Capital cities are where a country's government meets. They usually began as ports or trading centers that grew successful and powerful.

Towns were built near a source of fresh water.

Industrial towns are usually near mines or ports.

Some towns grow up where people go for holidays. These are called holiday resorts.

8. Which one of these is not a capital city: a) Rome; b) Paris; c) New York; d) Wellington?

9. Capital cities are always found in the middle of a country. True or false?

10. Does a new town nowadays need to be built near farms and rivers for food and water?

11. Which one of the towns above would have had most difficulty finding fresh water?

What is a shanty town?

Shanty towns are areas in some cities where the poorest people live. Homes are made from scrap materials like cardboard boxes and corrugated iron. These homes will probably have no gas, drains, electricity or clean water supply. Six or more people may share two small rooms and diseases spread quickly. In Lima, the capital of Peru, one in six people lives in a shanty town.

People come to cities such as Lima when they cannot find work in the countryside. They live in shanty towns if they are unable to find a job and a home.

12. Another name for a shanty town is: a) a barriada; b) a boom town; c) a new town.

13. Which continent is Peru in?

Lima has expensive homes too. There is a great difference in the lives of the rich and poor.

14. In some cities homeless children live in sewers. True or false?

Did you know?

The underground trains in Tokyo are so crowded that special "pushers" are employed to squeeze people into the carriages.

15. Tokyo is the capital city of: a) Mexico; b) Australia; c) Japan.

Spaces and wild places

The empty areas of the earth are almost always hot, cold or high. Very few people live in these places, but those that do have learned how to cope with the extreme conditions.

Many of these people have lived in the same way for thousands of years. This is changing, though. Nowadays, large companies are moving into these areas to look for minerals such as oil, gas and coal. Many wild places can also be turned into farmland.

Who lives in the mountains?

There is less oxygen the higher up you go. The Quecha Indians live 12,000ft (3,650m) up in the South American Andes. They have bigger hearts and lungs than people living at sea level. These can carry more blood and therefore more oxygen.

1. What are these flat sections cut into the mountainside used for?

2. The Quecha Indians use llamas for: a) transport; b) pets; c) bed warmers.

Llamas

3. Quecha Indians can walk barefoot over icy rocks without feeling cold. True or false?

Beans and potatoes are tough enough to grow in cold places.

Where are the coldest places?

The coldest places on earth are the areas within the Arctic and Antarctic Circles around the North and South Poles.

Who lives in the Antarctic?

The continent of Antarctica is covered by a layer of ice two miles (about three or four kilometers) thick. It is too cold for anyone to live a normal life here. Scientists come to study the wildlife or carry out experiments on the air, which is very pure. They live in homes built under the snow, away from the fierce winds and cold.

Outside, the average temperature is −58°F (−50°C).

Entrance

Inside it is 68°F (20°C).

Double door with airlock.

4. Palm trees grow on the coast of Antarctica. True or false?

5. Are polar bears a danger to Antarctic scientists?

Who lives in the Arctic?

Some people live just inside the Arctic circle. The Inuit, for instance, live in northern Canada, Alaska and Greenland. It is warmer here than in Antarctica because inside most of the Arctic Circle is ocean, which is warmer than land. Near the North Pole, though, the Arctic Ocean is frozen solid.

6. Which one of these countries does not have land inside the Arctic Circle: a) Greenland; b) Canada; c) Scotland?

7. Do the Inuit all live in igloos?

These traditional Inuit clothes are made of animal skins. Many Inuit now wear clothing made from man-made materials.

Thick skin jacket.

Thick sealskin or reindeer skin trousers.

Strong sealskin boots stuffed with dry grass.

The Inuit are mostly short and stocky. This helps them to keep warm as there is less body area exposed to the cold than in tall, long-limbed people. Many Inuit now work in the local oil and gas industries instead of making a living by hunting and fishing in the traditional way.

Who lives in deserts?

Deserts are areas with little or no rain. People who live in them have to be able to survive when there is very little food or water. The San of the Kalahari desert live by hunting animals and gathering plants.

The San live in small groups of 20 people or less. They camp for only a few weeks in one place. From each camp they hunt and gather over an area of 230 sq miles (600 sq km). Nowadays, much of the San's richer land has been taken over by wealthy cattle ranchers.

The San make cloaks, called karosses, from animal skins to keep them warm at night.

They have few possessions to carry with them.

8. Is it hot or cold at night in the desert?

The San search for water-filled plants such as tsama melons. These may be the only source of water for up to nine months of the year. San women's bodies adapt themselves so that they do not get pregnant when there is a drought.

Tsama melons

The San eat every scrap of meat killed in a hunt. They can store more fat on their bodies than most people.

The San hunt with bows and arrows.

9. In droughts, San only hunt male animals. True or false?

Did you know?

The San store water in ostrich eggshells. They sometimes bury the shells, so that they can use the water when rivers and water holes dry up. The eggshells are ½in (around 1cm) thick, so they are quite tough.

10. Which are bigger, ostrich eggs or hen eggs?

What is a tropical rainforest?

Tropical rainforests grow near the Equator where it is very hot and wet. They are the home of nearly half the world's different kinds of plants and animals.

The soil in a rainforest is kept rich by dead leaves and rotting wood from the trees. If the forest is cut down the soil loses its goodness and can no longer be used for growing crops. People who live in the forest survive by looking after it.

11. About two million different kinds of plants and animals live in rainforests. True or false?

Who lives in the rainforest?

The Mbuti pygmies of Central Africa live by hunting wild animals and gathering edible plants. They move from place to place in search of food. They do no damage to the forest.

12. Are pygmies short or tall people?

13. Which people have a bigger choice of food, the San or the Mbuti?

Women and girls build houses. They cover a stick framework with a layer of large leaves.

Honey **Nuts**

Yam

14. A yam is a vegetable which tastes like: a) a potato; b) a carrot; c) a cabbage.

15. It takes about: a) a week; b) a day; c) five minutes to build a pygmy house.

Nowadays, the forest is being cleared for farmland and timber. This is taking away land from the pygmies. Many now work as farm laborers in villages at the edge of the forest.

Using the land

Two out of three people on earth live and work on farms. They grow food, or crops such as rubber and cotton. The land is farmed in many different ways. Some people only grow enough to feed themselves and their families. Others have huge areas of land where crops such as wheat are grown. These crops are sold to large companies who then sell them all over the world.

1. Which two of the following are made from wheat: a) corn flakes; b) bread; c) spaghetti; d) rice pudding?

2. Which one of the following foods is not farmed: a) beef; b) trout; c) apples; d) tuna; e) rice?

Who are the small farmers?

Most farms in poor countries are small. Many people only have enough land to grow food for themselves. Some farmers also keep farms small to protect the soil. In tropical rainforests, for example, the soil would be destroyed if large areas of forest were cut to make fields.

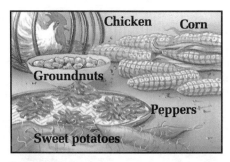

The Yanomami of South America clear small gardens in the tropical rainforest. Some trees are left to protect the soil. After two or three years the garden is left to return to forest and a new area is cleared.

3. Sometimes a Yanomamo person is eaten by monkeys. True or false?

The Tuareg of the Sahara keep herds of camels and goats, to provide them with milk and meat. They need to travel from place to place to find enough food to feed their animals.

4. The Sahara is a huge desert in South America. True or false?

On some small farms, the farmers grow more than they need to feed themselves. They sell the extra at local markets. The picture shows the kinds of food you could buy in a Nigerian market.

5. In which continent is Nigeria?

Why are some farms so big?

In richer countries, where most people work in towns and cities, farmland is likely to be owned by only a few farmers. Most of these farms cover large areas of land. Some farms grow a single type of crop, or keep just one breed of animal. In the USA, grain is grown in huge fields. Expensive machines do most of the work and very few people work on the farm.

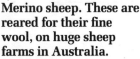

Wheat farm in central USA.

Merino sheep. These are reared for their fine wool, on huge sheep farms in Australia.

6. The farm machine shown above is: a) a combine harvester; b) a plough; c) a crop sprayer.

7. Are there more sheep farmers or sheepshearers in Australia?

Some Australian sheep farms are so huge that farmers travel around their farms in small planes.

8. Which of these countries is also well-known for its sheep: a) Peru; b) New Zealand; c) Finland?

What is a plantation?

Plantations are large estates where one crop, such as coffee, cocoa, tea or rubber, is grown. Most plantation crops need to be picked by hand, and many people work on plantations for low wages.

More than one third of the farmland in poor countries is used for plantations. They produce crops to be sold to other countries. Many plantation workers have their own plot of land to grow food for themselves.

9. Bananas grow underground. True or false?

10. Which of these countries is not a major tea producer: a) China; b) India; c) Belgium?

Cocoa beans are used to make chocolate.

Tea leaves are picked by hand.

Coffee beans are inside coffee berries.

Where does your food come from?

The food you eat comes from all over the world. Different kinds of food need different kinds of climate. Coffee grows well in Brazil and Kenya, for example. These countries usually have a very hot climate and a lot of rain. Apples, though, like a warm climate, as in France, and medium amounts of rain. The map below shows some examples of where your food might come from.

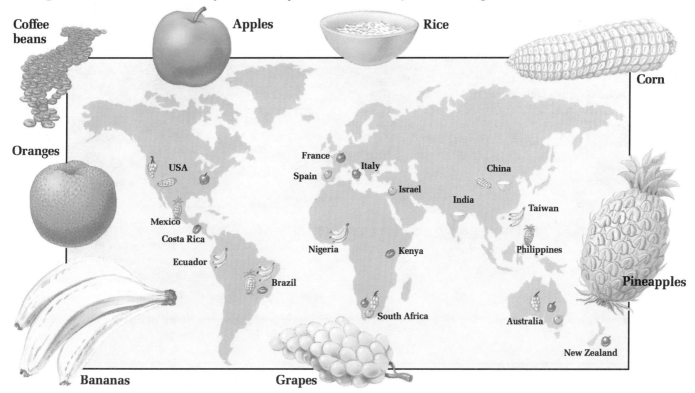

Coffee beans · Apples · Rice · Corn · Oranges · USA · France · Italy · Spain · Israel · China · India · Taiwan · Mexico · Costa Rica · Nigeria · Kenya · Philippines · Ecuador · Brazil · South Africa · Australia · New Zealand · Pineapples · Bananas · Grapes

11. Can bananas be farmed in parts of Europe?

12. Are there farms in all seven continents?

13. Do dates grow best in warm or cold countries?

Did you know?

Potatoes and many other common foods were unknown in Europe until the sixteenth century. Explorers brought them back from the mountains in the northern Andes, in South America. Explorers also brought tobacco, tomatoes and chillies from America to Europe.

14. South American Indians worshipped the potato. True or false?

15. Which one of these is not needed in a balanced diet: a) carbohydrate; b) protein; c) meat; d) vitamins; e) minerals?

Fuel and energy

Anything that lives or moves needs energy. A car needs fuel to drive its engine. You need food to give your body energy.

Energy in fuels such as coal, oil and gas can be converted into electricity by burning and processing them in power stations. You can use this electricity for lighting, heating, cooking and many other things. Most ways of producing electricity cause pollution,* and new ways are being developed that are cleaner and safer.

How was coal made?

About 300 million years ago large areas of the Earth were covered in hot, wet, tropical swamps.

As plants died, they collected in the bottom of the swamps.

Over millions of years, layers of sand and clay settled on top. They pressed down and hardened into rocks.

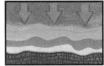

The pressure from the rocks gradually changed the plants into peat and then into coal.

When coal is burned, it produces gases that make the air dirty. This is called air pollution (see pages 24-25).

1. Is coal found only underground?

2. Do trees contain energy?

What are fossil fuels?

Fossil fuels are fuels such as coal and oil which are found buried below the land and sea. They are made from the remains of animals and plants which lived millions of years ago. They contain energy which was stored by the animals and plants when they were alive.

3. Which of these is not a fossil fuel: a) oil; b) wood; c) coal?

When will fossil fuels run out?

Fossil fuels will not last forever. The world's coal supplies will probably run out in about 400 years. Oil and gas supplies will probably run out by the middle of the next century. There are plenty of energy sources on earth besides fossil fuels. Some of them are shown below.

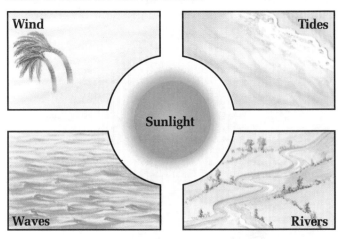

You can see how the energy is released from these sources on the next page. This sort of energy is called renewable or free energy because it will never run out.

4. Where is natural gas found?

5. Oil is found underground in: a) oil mines; b) oil wells; c) oil barrels.

What is nuclear energy?

You, and everything in the world, are made from atoms. Atoms are so tiny that there are more atoms in an ant than there are people in the world. Nuclear energy is made from splitting the atoms of a metal called uranium. When the center, or nucleus, is split, heat is given off. This can be used to make electricity.

6. A piece of uranium the size of a pin contains as much energy as 5,000 tons (tonnes) of coal. True or false?

7. Put these in order of discovery: a) steam power; b) nuclear power; c) electricity.

This picture shows how an atom is split.

A tiny particle, called a neutron, is fired at the uranium nucleus.

Uranium nucleus

What is the energy of the future?

The pictures below show several ways of supplying energy which do not depend on fossil fuels.

Solar panel

Windmill

Windmill blades turn turbines to make electricity. One hundred windmills could provide enough electricity for 400,000 people.

Solar panels trap the Sun's heat. This heats water to make steam to run turbines in power stations. Solar power can also be used to heat houses.

8. It costs nothing to convert free energy into electricity. True or false?

Tidal power dam

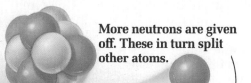

The movement of the tide can be used to turn turbines and make electricity, by building a tidal power dam across an estuary.

9. Is tidal power made inland or by the sea?

10. Do bicycles, skateboards and horse-drawn carts need fuel to make them move?

11. Which is the best source of energy for hot desert countries?

12. Which one of these uses energy from water: a) steam train; b) yacht; c) aircraft?

13. Which is the best source of energy for flat, windy countries?

Are there other energy sources?

These sources of energy are also being developed.

 Biogas is a gas made from rotting animal, plant and human waste. A small farm can provide itself with enough biogas to cook with.

 There is a lot of heat energy inside the earth. In Iceland and New Zealand, hot springs heat homes and make electricity.

 Chains of rafts around a coastline absorb the energy of waves and turn it into electricity.

 The power in falling water can be used to make electricity.

14. What is electricity made from the power in falling water called?

 Many kinds of household and industrial rubbish, which is usually buried, can be burned, and the heat used to make electricity. This also gets rid of the rubbish. However, burning rubbish does cause air pollution.

More neutrons are given off. These in turn split other atoms.

The nucleus is split and heat is given off.

Neutrons

When an atom is split, it sends harmful, invisible rays into the air. This is called radiation. It can cause burns and cancer. The waste from nuclear fuel is also radioactive (it gives off harmful radiation). No one has yet found a completely safe way to get rid of this waste.

Did you know?

It is possible to run a car on alcohol. In Brazil, an alcohol called ethanol is made from sugar cane. Ethanol burns easily and can be used for fuel in cars with modified engines. In 1990 a third of all cars in Brazil ran on ethanol.

15. Cars can also run on cow dung. True or false?

Pollution

When air, water or land is made dirty or poisonous it is described as polluted. A polluted environment can be very harmful to the people, animals and plants within it.

1. Which of these cause pollution: a) planes; b) bicycles; c) cars; d) sailboats?

What is acid rain?

Acid rain is made when poisonous gases and smoke in the air mix with water droplets in the clouds. This makes weak acids which fall to the ground as acid rain. This is sour, like vinegar, and it can kill plants and fish. The pictures below show where most of the poisonous gases that make acid rain come from.

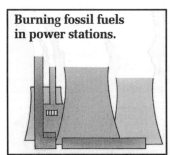
Burning fossil fuels in power stations.

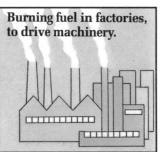
Burning fuel in factories, to drive machinery.

Exhaust fumes from cars, trucks and buses.

Burning fuel for cooking and heating in homes.

2. Is there such a thing as acid snow?

3. Can you name two ways of producing electrical energy which do not pollute the air?

What is the ozone layer?

Ozone is a gas that occurs 10-30 miles (20-50km) above the ground and forms a protective layer around the earth.

6. Is the ozone layer above or below where the weather happens?

Ozone protects the earth from dangerous light rays, called ultraviolet light, in sunlight. Too much ultraviolet light can cause skin cancer and eye diseases as well as damaging food crops, fish and other sea life.

7. Ultraviolet light can turn your skin purple. True or false?

The ozone layer is being damaged by gases called CFCs (short for chlorofluorocarbons, pronounced kloro-floro-carbons). These are used in things like foam boxes for take-away food, and in refrigerators and air-conditioning units. When these things break down or are destroyed, CFCs are released into the atmosphere.

Scientists have discovered two huge holes in the ozone layer – one over the Antarctic as big as the USA and another over the Arctic as big as Greenland.

8. Which of these might contain CFCs: a) cereal packet; b) hamburger carton; c) paper bag?

Ozone layer wraps around the earth.

Hole in ozone layer

Ultra-violet rays

What harm does acid rain do?

Clouds containing acid rain may be carried more than 1,000km (over 600 miles) by the wind. The acid rain then falls a long way from the city, factory or power station which caused it. Acid rain can affect the environment in several ways, as shown in the pictures below.

Acid rain damages plants and crops. It removes the richness from the soil so crops cannot grow well.

Acid rain attacks leaves on trees. Half of western Germany's forests are dying due to acid rain.

Acid rain pollutes water. About 4,000 lakes in Sweden now have no fish due to poisoning by acid rain.

Acid rain eats away at buildings. It is a particularly damaging type of air pollution. An Ancient Greek temple called the Parthenon has been worn down more in the last 30 years than in the last 2,000.

4. The Parthenon is in: a) Rome; b) Athens; c) Cairo?

5. The Parthenon is made of concrete. True or false?

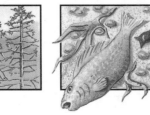

Acid rain eats into buildings.

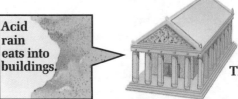
The Parthenon

What is the greenhouse effect?

A certain kind of air pollution is making the earth's atmosphere act like a greenhouse. It is making the earth's temperature rise very slowly. The sun warms up the earth but the atmosphere does not let the heat escape into space. This is called the greenhouse effect. It is also called global warming.

9. Only green plants grow in greenhouses. True or false?

The main cause of global warming is too much carbon dioxide in the atmosphere. Fossil fuels give off carbon dioxide when they are burned. Power stations which use coal are big producers of carbon dioxide. Fumes from car exhausts and CFCs also add to global warming.

10. Carbon dioxide in the atmosphere acts like the: a) glass; b) plants; c) air in a greenhouse.

11. Which one of these can help stop global warming: a) planting forests; b) burning fossil fuels; c) building greenhouses?

Sun's rays

Carbon dioxide acts like a greenhouse around the earth.

In a greenhouse, the sun shines through the glass and heats the air. The glass stops most of the heat from leaving the greenhouse.

Why is global warming a problem?

If the world heats up by just a few degrees, some of the ice around the North and South Poles will melt. The extra water in the oceans will make sea levels slowly rise all over the world. Cities such as London and New York could disappear under the sea. Low-lying countries like Holland and Bangladesh could disappear completely.

The pictures on the left show how the map of Western Europe would change if all the ice at the poles were to melt. The sea would rise by 200 ft (61m).

13. Which two of these could cause flooding in a country: a) tidal waves; b) monsoon rain; c) severe drought; d) overflowing baths?

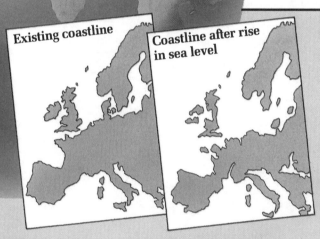

Existing coastline

Coastline after rise in sea level

12. Would you use a physical or a political map to work out how a rise in sea level would affect the land?

Did you know?

If a plastic bottle is dumped in the countryside, it will stay there for ever. Sunlight will decompose the plastic a little but once the bottle is buried in the ground it will not rot any more.

14. Which one of these everyday items cannot be made out of plastic: a) reading glasses; b) raincoat; c) ham sandwich; d) carpet; e) carrier bag?

15. Which of these words means "to use again": a) recycle; b) reset; c) reserve?

How can pollution be reduced?

Here are some of the ways you can help to reduce pollution.

Use less electricity. Switch off lights and heaters when you do not need them.

If you have a short journey, walk instead of travelling by car.

These will help reduce gases which cause acid rain and global warming.

Use detergents that do not contain phosphate cleaning chemicals.

Use smaller amounts of dishwashing soap and bathroom cleaner.

All these cleaners pollute water.

Make sure that all your garbage goes in the trashcan, not in the street or countryside. If you can, buy glass or aluminum containers rather than plastic, and recycle them.

Glass and aluminum can be broken down and reused. Many plastics are indestructible.

Geography Megaquiz

These ten quizzes test you on what you have read in Part One of this book and also on your general knowledge of geography.

You can write your answers on a piece of paper and then check on page 32 to see how many you got right

Capitals and countries

Can you match the capital cities in the purple strip to the countries in the blue strip?

Canada	New Zealand	India	Denmark	Argentina	USA	Australia	China	Spain	Peru
Delhi	Copenhagen	Buenos Aires	Ottawa	Wellington	Beijing	Madrid	Lima	Washington DC	Canberra

Earth facts

1. Which is the largest ocean?
2. Which is the most southern continent?
3. Latitude and longitude lines are found: a) on the sides of mountains; b) on maps; c) on fishing boats.
4. Which is the thinnest layer of the earth: a) the crust; b) the mantle; c) the core?
5. How long does it take for the earth to spin around once on its axis?
6. Glaciers are frozen: a) lakes; b) waterfalls; c) rivers.
7. Are tropical rainforests getting larger or smaller?
8. Is more of the earth covered by sea or by land?
9. Where might you find phytoplankton: a) in the sea; b) under the ground; c) in the atmosphere?
10. What is the name of latitude 0°?

Seas and oceans

Can you match the seas and oceans in the list below with the areas marked a – j on the map?

Atlantic Ocean
Southern Ocean
Indian Ocean
Pacific Ocean
Black Sea

North Sea
Arctic Ocean
South China Sea
Arabian Sea
Mediterranean Sea

People and places

Can you match the people described below to the shaded places on the map?

1. The first people on earth probably lived here, according to scientists.
2. People here currently have the longest lives.
3. The Tuareg live in this desert.
4. The Inuit live here.
5. The San live in this desert.
6. The Yanomami live in this rainforest.
7. The Quecha Indians live in these mountains.
8. People in this country form the largest population.
9. People crossed from Asia to this continent 12,000 years ago.
10. Over a fifth of the world can speak the language of the people from this country.

Close-ups

These are all close-ups of pictures in Part One. Can you recognize what they are?

1.

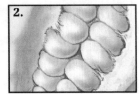
2.

3.

4.

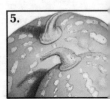
5.

26

Countries and continents

Match the pictures of countries and continents labelled a – j to the list of places below.

Australia   Japan   South America
Italy   Canada   Antarctica
Greece   Norway   Africa
India

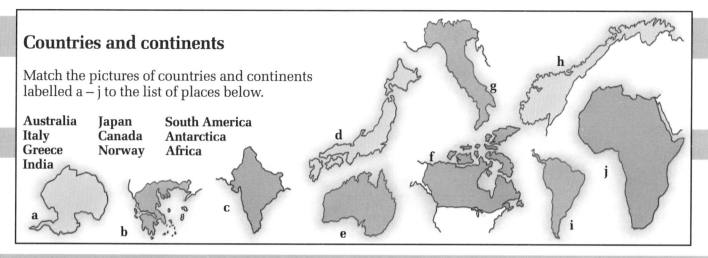

The sky and beyond

1. The first person landed on the moon in:
   a) 1928; b) 1969; c) 1989.
2. The moon takes about: a) a day; b) a week;
   c) a month to circle the earth.
3. Which part of the environment do CFCs harm:
   a) the ozone layer; b) the sea; c) the soil?
4. Which planet is closest to the sun?
5. Does lightning make the air it goes through hot
   or cold?
6. Is the sun: a) a planet; b) a star; c) an
   asteroid?
7. Which is bigger, the universe or our solar
   system?
8. Which of these is not usually found in the air:
   a) oxygen; b) nitrogen; c) plutonium?
9. What is a mixture of falling ice and rain called?
10. Which is bigger, a hurricane or a tornado?

Misfits

In each set of three below, there is one misfit. Can you spot which it is?

1. Jupiter; Saturn; the moon.
2. Brazil; Tokyo; Sweden.
3. Mediterranean; Pacific; Atlantic.
4. Tornado; hurricane; lightning.
5. Quecha; San; Merino.
6. Wood; coal; oil.
7. Wave power; wind power; nuclear power.
8. Cirrus; axis; stratus.
9. Alabama; Andes; Alps.
10. Sahara; Kalahari; Nairobi.

Silhouettes

All these silhouettes are of things that appear in Part One. How many can you recognize?

1.   2.   3.   4.   5.   6.   7.   8.   9.   10.

True or false?

1. The moon circles around the earth.
2. Some mountain people have bigger hearts and lungs
   than people living at sea level.
3. Saturn's rings are made of gold.
4. Scientists have travelled to the center of the earth.
5. Most of the people in the world live or work on
   farms.
6. A country is a small continent.
7. Thunder is caused by two clouds bumping into each
   other.
8. The earth is travelling through space at nearly
   18.6 miles (30km) per second.
9. Some cars can run on sugar.
10. Asteroids are a drug for fattening cattle.

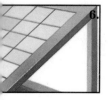 6.  7.  8. 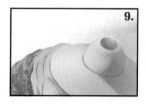 9.  10.

Quiz answers

The answers to the 12 quizzes from *The earth in space* to *Pollution* are on the next four pages. Give yourself one point for every right answer. The chart below helps you find out how well you have done in each quiz.

0-5	Read through the answers, then try the quiz again. See how many answers you can remember second time around.	11-14	Good score. If you get this score on most of the quizzes, you have done very well.
6-10	Quite good. Think more carefully about the questions and you might get more answers right.	15	Excellent. If you do this well in more than half the quizzes, you are a geography genius!

Your score overall

You can find out your average score over all 12 quizzes like this:

1. Add up your scores on all 12 quizzes.
2. Divide this total by 12. This is your average score. How well did you do?

General knowledge

All the answers to general knowledge questions are marked★. These questions are probably the hardest in the quizzes. Add up how many of them you got right across all 12 quizzes. There are 50 of them in total. If you got over 30 right, your geography general knowledge is good.

The earth's atmosphere

1. c) A solar system is made up of a star and circling planets.
★ 2. No. The earth is just one tiny planet in one of millions of galaxies.
★ 3. a) light years. A light year is the distance a ray of light would travel in a year — 5,878 thousand million miles (9,460 thousand million km).
4. No. Stars give off light and heat. The moon only reflects sunlight.
★ 5. b) Neil Armstrong was the first man on the moon, in July 1969.

Neil Armstrong's landing craft.

6. Pluto is the coldest planet, as it is the furthest (3,700 million miles or 5,900 million km) from the sun.
★ 7. Venus is named after the Roman goddess of love.
8. The Milky Way is much bigger than a solar sytem.
9. JUPITER and MARS.
10. In the picture when it is day in Africa it is night in South America.
11. True. In July the top of the earth is tilting towards the sun. The North Pole never moves into the area of shadow.

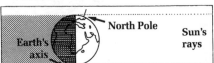
North Pole · Earth's axis · Sun's rays

12. False. All parts of the world have 24 hours in a day.
13. No. In our solar system, Mercury and Venus do not have moons.
14. No. Neptune is a very cold planet with a poisonous, frozen atmosphere. Nothing could survive there.
15. No. You cannot see a New Moon because the side of it that is lit up is facing away from the earth.

The surface of the earth

1. The Arctic and Antarctic would be white or bluish-white. They are both covered with ice and snow.
★ 2. The largest continent is Asia.

Asia · **Australia is the smallest continent.**

3. No. Nobody lives at the North Pole. It is in the frozen Arctic Ocean.
4. False. Cold weather and steep slopes make mountains difficult to farm.
★ 5. The Himalayas are in Asia.
6. There are many more penguins than people at the Antarctic.
7. True. The Sahara desert covers almost all of northern Africa.
8. b) The River Nile flows through Egypt.
9. True. Around two-thirds of Brazil is covered by the Amazon rainforest.

Amazon rainforest

★10. The center of the earth is much hotter than the Sahara desert. It is probably about 11,000°F (6,000°C) at the center of the earth — over one hundred times hotter than any temperature recorded on land.
★11. True. Africa and South America used to be joined together. They began to separate about 135 million years ago.
12. a) The lowest places on earth are at the bottom of the sea. The lowest place known is the Marianas Trench which is more than 36,000ft (11,000m) below sea level.
13. b) San Francisco is famous for its earthquakes.
★14. Yes. Volcanoes can erupt under the sea as well as on land.
★15. Mount Everest. It is 29,028ft (8,848m) high.

Mapping the world

1. A globe is more accurate than a flat map of the earth. Mapmakers do not need to change the shape of the land and sea to make a globe.

Globe

★ 2. Asia is the missing continent.
3. You would use a political map to find a country's borders. Political maps usually also show the position of major cities.
4. There are 13 countries in South America. These are: Argentina; Bolivia; Brazil; Chile; Columbia; Ecuador; French Guiana; Guyana; Paraguay; Peru; Surinam; Uraguay and Venezuela.
5. No. There is not a West Pole (or an East Pole).
★ 6. The direction half way between north and east is north-east.
★ 7. South is the direction at the bottom of most maps.
8. No. Latitude and longitude lines are only found on maps.
9. c) London. Longitude 0° runs through an astronomy museum, called the Royal Observatory, and is marked on the floor with an iron bar.

Greenwich Royal Observatory

10. The ships are nearer to Europe.
11. The volcano's position is 40°N, 20°E.
12. The hurricane's position is 20°N 60°W.
13. There is flat land on the map at C.
14. It is very steep at B.
15. A is at the top of a hill.

The earth's atmosphere

★ 1. You need to breathe oxygen.
2. Yes. Jets cruise above most weather, but still have to fly through bad weather when they take off and land.
★ 3. b) At 0 miles (0km) it is sea level. This is the same everywhere, unlike land with its mountains and valleys.
4. True. There is less air above you on top of a mountain than there is at sea level, so air pressure is less.
★ 5. It is hot at the Equator. The sun's rays are most concentrated here.

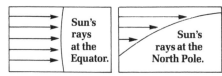

★ 6. a) A weather vane tells you which way the wind is blowing.

Weather vane

7. False. It is warmer at sea level than on the top of a mountain. This is because the sun's rays have more land surface area to heat in mountainous areas than in flat ground and sea. Also, air holds heat, and the higher you go, the less air there is to hold it.

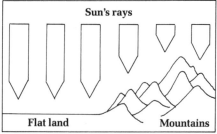

Sun's rays

Flat land   Mountains

8. Great Britain has more changeable weather than the Sahara desert, which is hot and dry all through the year.
9. No. Climate is the kind of weather a place has on average year after year. Weather is what a place has from day to day.
10. Cirrus clouds are the highest clouds. They are found at around 11 miles (18km) up in the sky.
★ 11. c) Smog is a mixture of smoke and fog.
12. The storm is 2 miles (about 4km) away if you hear thunder ten seconds after seeing lightning.
13. There are more thunderstorms at the Equator. Weather here is far more changeable, with plenty of the hot air currents thunderstorms need.
14. True. The center of a hurricane is called the eye. The eye is a calm area with no wind.
15. False. Tornadoes have never been known to lift trains right off the ground. They can, however, turn over trains and grounded aircraft.

Rivers and rain

1. a) Camels can survive without a drink for 21 days (three weeks) if they only eat dry food. If they eat succulent desert plants which contain water, they never need to drink.

Desert plant

2. b) The water in wet washing becomes water vapor when it dries.
3. Clouds are made of water. Most clouds are made of tiny water droplets, but high cirrus clouds have tiny ice crystals in them.
4. True. In fact all the water in the world is constantly being recycled.
5. Yes. Your breath contains water vapor. You can see the water in your breath when you breathe out on a cold day.
★ 6. a) The Thames (215 miles/346km) is much shorter than either the Nile (4145 miles/6670km) or Amazon (4007 miles/6448km). The Nile is the longest river in the world.

Relative length of rivers:

Thames —

Amazon ————————————

Nile   ————————————

7. False. Rivers can only flow downhill.
★ 8. Water freezes at 32°F (0°C).
9. b) You can live without water for four days.
10. False. Hydroelectric power stations are often found in mountainous regions where fast flowing water drives the power station turbines.
11. Hydroelectric, tidal and wave power are all forms of water power.
★ 12. b) The Grand Canyon is not a famous waterfall. It is a deep, steep-sided valley, cut by the Colorado River in the USA.

The Grand Canyon

13. True. Fish caught from polluted rivers and eaten can cause stomach upsets or more serious poisoning.
14. c) Glaciers are found in Scandinavia. Glaciers are also found in many other parts of the world, such as India,
15. Rivers flow a lot quicker than glaciers. Glaciers only move an inch or two (a few centimeters) a day, so slowly that you cannot see them move.

Oceans and coasts

1. Yes. The earth's oceans are all joined together.
2. c) The Mediterranean is a sea.

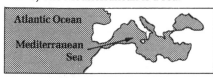

★ 3. Yes. Seawater evaporates in shallow pools and salt is left behind.
4. True. Seawater contains a tiny amount of gold.
5. True. In big storms, cliffs can form overnight. In 1953 at Covehithe in England the coast was cut back 90ft (27m) in a day.
6. False. Cliffs can also be found along river banks where the river has worn away the valley in its path.
★ 7. a) A starling is not a seabird.
8. Sand dunes are found on beaches. They occur when the wind usually blows in the direction of the shore and sand is blown up the beach.

Wind   Sand dune

9. c) You can see about one eighth of an iceberg above the water.

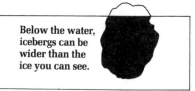

Below the water, icebergs can be wider than the ice you can see.

★ 10. The Titanic. This luxury passenger liner was travelling from England to the USA. When the Titanic sank, over 1,500 people drowned.
11. a) An octopus will try to escape from an enemy in a cloud of black ink. The octopus carries this ink, called sepia, in a special sac in its body. Artists have used sepia in paintings since Roman times.
12. Yes, seaweed such as laver, dulse, and sea lettuce can be eaten.

Edible seaweed

★ 13. Three of these animals are fish – the mackerel, cod and angler fish.
14. True. Many deep sea fish have parts of their bodies which light up. The light comes from luminous bacteria, which live in the fish. These lights attract prey to eat, and also other deep sea fish to mate with.
15. True. Dolphins are small streamlined whales.

People around the world

1. Japanese people are of the Mongolian race.
2. Scandinavian people are of the Caucasian race.
3. c) The first humans might have hunted antelope in the African grassland.
4. b) No one lives permanently in Antarctica because it is too cold.

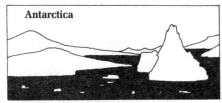

Antarctica

5. True. About one in five people on earth is Chinese.
6. People arrived in China first. There have been people in China for at least 70,000 years. Scientists think that people only reached South America around 11,000 years ago.
★ 7. The original inhabitants of Australia are called Aborigines.
8. True. Around 400,000 babies are born every day. Around 150,000 people die every day too, so each day there are 250,000 more people on earth.

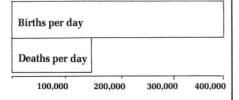

Births per day			
Deaths per day			
100,000	200,000	300,000	400,000

9. The tennis racket and the books do not need electricity. Electrical power has only been widely available since the beginning of this century.
10. b) Throughout the world the average number of children in a family is four.
11. b) Food and water are essential for survival.
★ 12. c) Shanghai is not a Chinese dish, it is a city in China. Beijing is China's capital city, but Shanghai is its biggest city, and largest port.

CHINA   Beijing•
        Shanghai•

★ 13. Afghanistan is in the continent of Asia.

EUROPE
        Afghanistan
            ASIA
AFRICA

★ 14. b) orange.
15. False. The Romans spoke Latin.

Cities and towns

★ 1. Dinosaurs lived on earth first. They died out about 65 million years ago. The first people lived on earth less than one million years ago.

Dinosaur

2. a) Rome was built first, over 2,500 years ago.
3. c) Village people might need to visit a town or city to buy a compact disc.
4. Cities would be cleaner and quieter if everyone came into them on buses and trains.
★ 5. The right order is train, motorbike, aircraft.

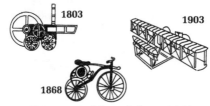

1803   1903

1868

6. Chicago would need about 6,000 tons (tonnes) of food every day.
7. False. Air pollution is mostly caused by industry, power stations burning fossil fuels, and cars.
8. c) New York. The capital of the USA is Washington DC.
9. False. Capital cities may be anywhere in a country. For example, Madrid, the capital of Spain, is in the center of the country, but Washington DC is on the east coast of the USA.

Madrid

Washington •
DC

10. No. Water can be piped and food transported over huge distances, so new towns can be built almost anywhere.
11. The town that has been built upon a hill to defend itself from enemies would have had the most difficulty finding fresh water.
12. a) A barriada is another name for a shanty town.
★ 13. Peru is in the continent of South America.

Pacific Ocean   Atlantic Ocean

Peru   SOUTH
        AMERICA

14. True. For example, in Brazil in South America, there are homeless children who live in sewers.
15. c) Tokyo is the capital city of Japan.

Spaces and wild places

★ 1. The flat sections cut into the mountainside are used for growing food. They are called terraces and they stop soil from being washed away.
2. a) The Quecha Indians use llamas for transport.
3. True. The Quechas' feet become toughened so they do not feel cold.
4. False. Palm trees only grow in warm climates.

Palm trees

★ 5. No. Polar bears do not live in the Antarctic. Like walruses, they are only found in the Arctic.
★ 6. c) Scotland does not have land within the Arctic Circle.
7. No. Very few Inuit still live in igloos, although some Inuit build them on winter hunting trips.

Igloo

8. It is cold at night in deserts. The temperature can drop below freezing.
9. True. In a drought the San take care not to hurt female and young animals so that some animals will survive for another time.
★ 10. Ostrich eggs are much bigger than hen eggs. An ostrich egg can be 8in (20cm) long and 6in (15cm) around.

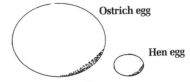

Ostrich egg

Hen egg

11. True. There are more varieties of plants and animals in tropical rainforests than anywhere else on earth.
★ 12. Pygmies are short people. Men in pygmy tribes are usually less than 5ft (150cm) tall.
13. The Mbuti have a bigger choice of food than the San. The rainforest provides the Mbuti with nuts, roots, vegetables and fungi, as well as termites, freshwater crabs and animals like antelope.
★ 14. a) A yam is a vegetable which tastes like a potato.

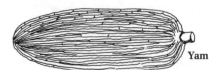

Yam

15. b) It takes about a day to make a pygmy house.

Using the land

1. b) and c). Bread and spaghetti are made from wheat.

Wheat

2. d) Tuna are not farmed. Tuna are fished from the open ocean, using large nets.
3. False. However, the Yanomami do sometimes eat monkeys.
4. False. The Sahara desert is a huge desert in Africa. It is about as big as the USA.
★ 5. Nigeria is in the continent of Africa.

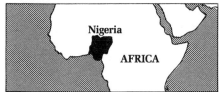

Nigeria

AFRICA

6. a) The farm machine shown in the picture is a combine harvester. Combine harvesters are used to cut wheat and other crops. They cut the straw and separate it from the grain. The grain is stored in the machine and the straw is dropped out of the back of the machine.
7. There are more shearers than sheep farmers in Australia. Each sheep is sheared by hand and shearers travel from farm to farm.
★ 8. b) New Zealand is also well-known for its sheep.
9. False. Bananas grow on huge herb plants which look like trees.

Banana plant

10. c) Belgium is not a major tea producer. Belgium is too cold for growing tea.
11. No. Bananas need a hot, wet, tropical climate to grow well.
12. No. There are no farms in Antarctica.
13. Dates grow best in warm countries.

Dates

14. False. South American Indians grew potatoes for food.
★ 15. c) Meat is not needed in a balanced diet. However, meat is a good source of protein, vitamins and minerals.

Fuel and energy

★ 1. No. Coal is not found only underground. Layers, or seams, of coal can be found on the surface and on the sides of hills. Collecting coal from these seams is called "open-cast mining."

Digger used in open-cast mining.

2. Yes. The energy in trees is released when they are burned for heating or cooking.
3. b) Wood is not a fossil fuel.
★ 4. Natural gas is found underground. It is often found with or near oil.

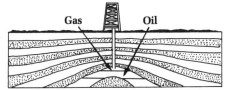

Gas   **Oil**

★ 5. b) Oil is found underground in oil wells.
6. True.
★ 7. Beginning with the earliest, the order is: a) steam power (early 18th century); c) electric power (late 19th century); b) nuclear power (mid-20th century).

Light bulb 1879

8. False. It is expensive to build power stations and turbines to convert free energy to electricity. Once completed, however, they are inexpensive to run.
9. Tidal power is made by the sea. A dam is usually built across a tidal river estuary.
★ 10. Yes. Even though skateboards, horse-drawn carts and bicycles do not use fuel, they still need energy. This comes from the food that the cyclist, skateboarder and horse eat.
11. The best source of energy for desert countries is solar energy, as the sun shines nearly all the time.
12. a) Steam trains convert water to steam, which powers their wheels.
13. Wind to drive windmills is the best source of energy for flat, windy countries.

Wind farm in California.

★ 14. This kind of electricity is called hydroelectricity.
15. False. Dried cow dung can be used, however, as a fuel for heating and cooking.

Pollution

1. a) and c). Plane and car engines burn fossil fuels, which cause pollution.
2. Yes. Acid snow is made in a similar way as acid rain.
★ 3. Give yourself a point if you got two of the following: hydroelectric power, wave power, tidal power, wind power, solar power, underground heat.
★ 4. b) The Parthenon is in Athens.

GREECE

Athens

5. False. The Parthenon was built of white marble, nearly two and a half thousand years ago.
6. The ozone layer is above where weather happens. (See page 8.)
7. False. Ultra-violet light will tend to make fair-skinned people browner.
8. b) A hamburger carton might contain CFCs.

Hamburger carton

9. False. Many kinds of different plants are grown in greenhouses.
10. a) Carbon dioxide in the atmosphere acts like the glass in a greenhouse.

Greenhouse

11. a) Planting forests can help to stop global warming. Trees, and other plants, take carbon dioxide from the air to give themselves energy, in a process called photosynthesis. They give off oxygen. Forests are very important on earth as they help to keep the correct balance of oxygen and carbon dioxide in the atmosphere.

Carbon dioxide   **Oxygen**

12. You would use a physical map to work out how a rise in sea level would affect the land.
13. a) and b) could cause flooding in a country.
14. c) A ham sandwich cannot be made out of plastic. Food is just about the only thing which cannot be made from plastic. Plastics can be used for almost everything else – from beach balls to aircraft fuselages.
★ 15. a) Recycle means "to use again."

Geography Megaquiz answers

There are 100 points in the Geography Megaquiz. If you score over 50 you have done well. Over 75 is excellent. You can find out more about the answers on the pages listed after them.

Capitals and countries

1. Canada/Ottawa.
2. New Zealand/Wellington.
3. India/Delhi.
4. Denmark/Copenhagen.
5. Argentina/Buenos Aires.
6. USA/Washington DC.
7. Australia/Canberra.
8. China/Beijing.
9. Spain/Madrid.
10. Peru/Lima.

Earth facts

1. The Pacific Ocean (page 4).
2. Antarctica (page 4).
3. b) on the maps (pages 6-7).
4. a) the crust (page 5).
5. A day – 24 hours (page 3).
6. c) rivers (page 11).
7. Smaller (page 19).
8. Sea (page 12).
9. a) in the sea (page 13).
10. The Equator (page 7).

Seas and oceans

1. Atlantic Ocean (d).
2. Southern Ocean (f).
3. Indian Ocean (h).
4. Pacific Ocean (b).
5. Black Sea (g).
6. North Sea (e).
7. Arctic Ocean (j).
8. South China Sea (c).
9. Arabian Sea (a).
10. Mediterranean Sea (i).

People and places

1. Central Africa (page 14).
2. Japan (page 15).
3. Sahara desert (page 20).
4. Greenland (page 18).
5. Kalahari desert (page 19).
6. South American rainforest (page 20).
7. Andes (page 18).
8. China (page 15).
9. North America (page 14).
10. England (page 15).

Close-ups

1. Windmill (page 23).
2. Cocoa beans (page 21).
3. Asteroids (page 2).
4. Contour lines (page 7).
5. Tsama melons (page 19).
6. Solar panel (page 23).
7. Eskimo clothes (page 18).
8. Merino sheep (page 20).
9. Chinese rice harvester (page 15).
10. City tower block (page 16).

Countries and continents

1. Australia (e).
2. Italy (g).
3. Greece (b).
4. India (c).
5. Japan (d).
6. Canada (f).
7. Norway (h).
8. South America (i).
9. Antarctica (a).
10. Africa (j).

The sky and beyond

1. b) 1969 (page 2).
2. c) a month (page 3).
3. a) the ozone layer (page 24).
4. Mercury (page 2).
5. Hot (page 9).
6. b) a star (page 2).
7. The universe (page 2).
8. c) plutonium (page 8).
9. Sleet.
10. A hurricane (page 9).

Misfits

1. The Moon is not a planet.
2. Tokyo is a city not a country.
3. The Mediterranean is not an ocean.
4. Lightning is not a wind.
5. Merino are sheep, not people.
6. Wood is not a fossil fuel.
7. Nuclear power is not "free" energy.
8. An axis is not a cloud.
9. Alabama is not a mountain range.
10. Nairobi is a city not a desert.

Silhouettes

1. Chopsticks (page 14).
2. Pineapple (page 21).
3. San bow and arrow (page 19)
4. Snowflake (page 8).
5. Bananas (page 21).
6. Research balloon (page 8).
7. Penguin (page 4).
8. Mbuti hut (page 19).
9. Cod (page 13).
10. Australian farm aircraft (page 20).

True or false?

1. True (page 3).
2. True (page 18).
3. False.
4. False
5. True (page 20).
6. False.
7. False.
8. True (page 3).
9. True (page 23).
10. False.

Place index

Below is a list of some of the places you can read about in Part One and where to look them up.

The photos on page 14 are reproduced by kind permission of the Hutchison Library.

Part Two

USBORNE FACTS & FUN ABOUT HISTORY

Alastair Smith

Edited by Judy Tatchell

Designed by
Nigel Reece and Richard Johnson

Illustrated by
Jonathon Heap and Peter Dennis

Additional illustration by
Kuo Kang Chen, Guy Smith and Steve Lings

Consultant: Julie Penn

Contents

About Part Two

Part Two of the book covers 12 topics from history. The
topics range from **The dinosaur age** to **The twentieth
century** and each one takes up two pages. There is lots
to read about all these topics, with quiz questions to
answer as you go along.

How to do the quizzes

Within each of the two-page topic sections there are 15 quiz questions for you to
answer. These questions are printed in italic type, *like this.* Some of the quiz
questions rely on general knowledge. Others ask you to guess whether a statement
is true or false, or to choose between several possible answers. You will be able to
answer some questions if you study the pictures on the page. Jot down your answers
on a piece of paper and check them against the correct answers on pages 60-63.

The History Megaquiz

On pages 58-59 is the **History Megaquiz.** This consists of
ten quick quizzes that ask questions about things you
have read about earlier in Part Two. Again, keep a note of
your answers and then check them against the **History
Megaquiz answers** on page 64.

The dinosaur age

Millions of years ago, strange reptiles called dinosaurs dominated the earth. They probably appeared about 210 million years ago and died out about 65 million years ago. Humans did not appear until about two million years ago.

Hundreds of different sorts of dinosaurs developed and then died out. Those on this page lived several million years before those opposite.

1. The word "dinosaur" means: a) terrible lizard; b) massive teeth; c) giant feet.

What was Earth like then?

When dinosaurs were alive, most of the land was fairly warm. There were swamps and oases scattered about. Dinosaurs and other reptiles liked these conditions.

2. Which dinosaur shown on these pages has a name which means Tyrant Lizard King?

3. What do you think this tail was used for?

4. Baby dinosaurs hatched from eggs laid in the sand. True or false?

Were all dinosaurs big?

Not all dinosaurs were big. Some, such as Compsognathus, were no bigger than large turkeys.

Stegosaurus was 23ft (7m) long – but its brain was only as big as a walnut.

Compsognathus

5. Bones preserved in rock are called: a) toggles; b) fossils; c) skulls.

Which was the biggest dinosaur?

The biggest dinosaur was called Brachiosaurus. It ate plants. It was longer than two buses and its footprints would have been big enough for you to sit down in.

6. Brachiosaurus was good at climbing trees. True or false?

Brachiosaurus

7. Nobody knows what color the dinosaurs were. True or false?

8. Which of these is not a reptile: a) alligator; b) Stegosaurus; c) hippopotamus?

Stegosaurus —

How did we get here?

The earth is about 4,600 million years old. Over time, its environment changes. Some living things adapt to changes. This is called evolution. Others do not adapt so they die out. This panel shows when different living things evolved.

9. Animal life began:
a) in the air;
b) in the sea;
c) on land.

3,000 million years ago.
Bacteria, the first life

1,500 million years ago.
Algae and jellyfish

500 million years ago.
Plants

280 million years ago.
Reptiles

200 million years ago.
Dinosaurs and mammals

Parasaurolophus' head was as long as a man.

10. Could any dinosaurs fly?

11. How many of the animals shown on these two pages still exist?

Which was the fiercest dinosaur?

Tyrannosaurus rex was the largest meat-eater that has ever lived. Its teeth were as long as daggers.

12. A meat-eater is called: a) a carnivore; b) a herbivore.

13. Was Tyrannosaurus rex the biggest dinosaur?

The top of Pachycephalosaurus' head was tougher than a brick. It was useful for butting enemies.

14. The number of different types of dinosaurs found so far is about: a) 6; b) 40; c) 800.

15. How many man-eating dinosaurs are shown on these two pages?

Tyrannosaurus rex

The first dinosaur fossil was found over 300 years ago. The finder thought it was a giant's bone.

How is a fossil made?

A dead animal's flesh rots away, leaving only the bony parts.

The bones are buried under mud, sand and rotting plants.

As pressure builds up on top of it, this earthy mixture turns to rock.

Rock

Over millions of years, the bones soak up minerals from the rock around them.

The bones become rock (fossilized). Fossils provide clues to what living things looked like long ago.

Why did the dinosaurs die out?

Nobody is certain why dinosaurs died out. A change in climate is the most likely reason. This would have led to a shortage of food.

This section shows how humans might have evolved from early sorts of ape.

35 million years ago. First apes

14 million years ago. Ramapithecus

5 million years ago. Man-ape

2 million years ago. Handy Man

1.5 million years ago. Upright Man

200 thousand years ago. Neanderthal Man

40 thousand years ago. Modern Man

Ancient Egypt

Thousands of years ago, the Ancient Egyptians built huge tombs, called pyramids, for their dead kings and queens. Some pyramids were taller than a 30-story building.

When a king or queen died, the Egyptians preserved the body. They thought this would mean that the dead person's spirit would live forever. They built a pyramid so that the spirit would always have a house on earth to return to.

By about 1550BC, the Ancient Egyptians had stopped building pyramids. Instead, they buried royalty in tombs cut out of the rock in a valley called the Valley of the Kings.

1. Is there still a country called Egypt?

2. Most of the pyramids have now sunk into the sand. True or false?

How was the body preserved?

To preserve the body, some organs were removed. The skin, bones and other remains were dried using a salty chemical. This took several weeks. Finally, the body was perfumed and bandaged in cloth. This process is called embalming.

The chief priest, dressed as Anubis, god of the dead, embalmed the body.

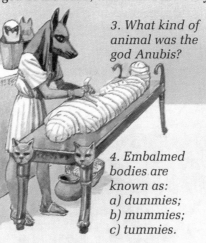

3. What kind of animal was the god Anubis?

4. Embalmed bodies are known as:
a) dummies;
b) mummies;
c) tummies.

5. The embalmed bodies of some Ancient Egyptians have lasted until today. True or false?

What was the funeral like?

The coffin was put onto a decorated sleigh and dragged to the tomb. The sleigh looked like a boat. The Egyptians thought the king would need a boat to cross the imaginary water between earth and heaven.

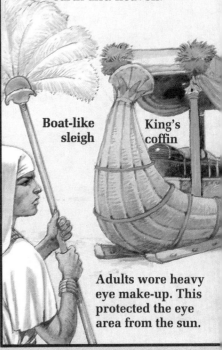

Boat-like sleigh

King's coffin

Adults wore heavy eye make-up. This protected the eye area from the sun.

How long did it take to build a pyramid?

It took 4,000 workers 20 years to build one of the biggest pyramids. The workers had to spend three months each year working on them.

The Egyptians wanted the pyramids to last forever. Only the best built pyramids are still completely standing today, though.

The Egyptians could have used more machinery but they built the pyramids mostly by hand. The harder the work, the more honor it did to the ruler. The Egyptians thought their kings were half god, half human.

The Egyptians built hundreds of statues like this, called sphinxes. The heads were carved to look like the heads of kings.

Ramps made of rubble and mud spiralled up around the pyramid. Builders dragged the huge stone blocks up these ramps.

7. Where was this stone, called a capstone going to be put?

Pyramids were covered with white limestone.

6. Which one was not a queen of Egypt: a) Cleopatra; b) Nefertiti; c) Elizabeth I?

Most adults shaved their hair and wore wigs. This was clean and cool.

Many children had shaved heads except for a single lock of hair.

Some girls had hair like dreadlocks.

8. A sphinx has the body of: a) a woman; b) a lion; c) a fish.

Did you know?

Tutankhamen became king when he was 10 and died aged 18. His tomb in the Valley of the Kings was discovered in 1922. Most other royal tombs had been robbed over the years but his was untouched.

10. What were Egyptian kings called?

11. Was Tutankhamen buried in a pyramid?

Some people believed that Tutankhamen's tomb was protected by a curse. The curse meant that anyone who entered the tomb would die. One of the people who found the tomb died a few weeks later. Some people thought this was due to the curse.

Tutankhamen's coffin was made of solid gold.

Where were other Egyptians buried?

Most people were buried in the sand on the outskirts of town. Embalming was so expensive that only rich people could afford it.

13. Unscramble the name of this Egyptian city: ariCo.

12. What did Egyptian children usually wear in the summer?

What was on the tomb walls?

The dead king was buried in here.

After the burial this passage was sealed.

Passages

False tombs might have been built to confuse grave robbers.

9. What made the pyramids white?

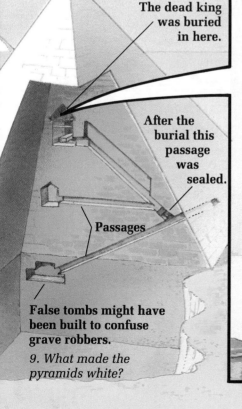

14. The symbols on the wall are called: a) anagrams; b) anaglypta; c) hieroglyphics.

Food, furniture and embalmed bodies of the king's pets.

15. Which of the symbols on the wall means "to walk"?

On the tomb walls were carved rows of pictures and symbols. This was a sort of writing. It told stories of the king's life and explained to his spirit how it should find its way to heaven.

Most of what we know about the Ancient Egyptians was discovered from picture-writing in pyramids and rock-cut tombs.

The coffin had a sculpture of the dead king's face on it.

Ancient Greece

About 2,500 years ago, Greece was made up of many cities. Each one ruled the countryside around it. What it was like to be alive then depended a lot on where you lived.

A wealthy person in the city of Athens, for instance, would have a comfortable life, with visits to the theatre and parties to go to. A young man in Sparta would be a soldier living in a grim barracks.

1. What is the capital of Greece now, Athens or Sparta?

What were Greek plays like?

You could watch two sorts of play in a Greek theatre. They were called tragedies and comedies. Women were not allowed to act so men had to dress up to play female roles.

Tragedies were about the fates of past Greek heroes and were serious. Actors wore masks to show the age, sex and mood of a character.

Comedies often made fun of politicians and important people.

2. What moods do these masks show?

3. Are Ancient Greek plays still performed today?

4. Greek actors used microphones so they could be heard. True or false?

Who was in charge of Athens?

Athens is famous for its system of government, called democracy. Each citizen could vote on how the city was run. Unfortunately, the Greeks did not allow women or slaves to be citizens, so they did not have a vote.

5. The word "democracy" means:
a) governed by the king; b) governed by the people;
c) governed by women.

Architects ever since have copied the elegant style of Ancient Greek buildings. The style is known as "classical."

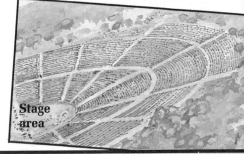

A political meeting

6. It was a crime to chop down an olive tree in Athens. True or false?

The ruin of this theatre is still standing in Athens. It held 14,000 people.

Stage area

Who was Homer?

Homer was a Greek poet who might have lived about 800BC. He made up long poems about mythical Greek heroes. Two of his poems, the *Iliad* and the *Odyssey*, have survived until now. The *Iliad* is about the legendary Trojan War.

7. Homer's poems were called:
a) epics; b) topics; c) episodes.

What was the Trojan War about?

A Trojan prince called Paris kidnapped Helen, the beautiful wife of Menelaus. Menelaus and his brother Agamemnon, a Greek king, raised an army and sailed to the city of Troy to fetch her back. There were 1,000 ships in the fleet that carried the army.

The Greeks besieged Troy for ten years without success. Then Odysseus, a Greek general, had a plan. The Greeks built a huge model horse and led the Trojans to believe it was a gift to the gods. They left the horse outside Troy and pretended to sail away.

8. Greece is part of which continent?

Who were the Greek gods?

The Greek gods behaved a bit like humans – they got jealous, argued and played tricks. However, they had magic powers so they could change shape, make things happen and get from one place to another in a flash.

12. Guess which god is which:
a) Poseidon, god of the sea;
b) Aphrodite, goddess of love;

c) Zeus, king of the gods;
d) Athene, goddess of wisdom.

How were children treated in Sparta?

Spartan boys were brought up to be the toughest soldiers in Greece. Girls also trained to be strong so they would have good warrior sons. The Spartans wanted to be able to resist any invasion or slave rebellion.

Boys were sent away to an army training school at the age of seven. They were taught to read and write but learning to use weapons was more important. They also had dancing lessons to make them strong and agile.

There is a story that the boys were underfed and had to steal extra food from local farms. If they were caught they were beaten by teachers – not for stealing, but for getting caught.

13. Before battle, Spartan soldiers put perfume in their hair. True or false?

Why were the Greeks keen on sport?

The Greeks were often at war. Fit, strong men made better soldiers so they exercised regularly at sports centers, called *gymnasia*.

14. Can you identify these four sports, all played by the Ancient Greeks?

Athletics festivals were held in stadiums like this.

Athletics festivals were held in honor of the gods. The most famous one was held every four years in the city of Olympia. People came from all over Greece to compete.

Did you know?

If the sports festival at Olympia started during a war, fighting was stopped so that soldiers could go and take part.

15. Which modern sports festival is named after the Games at Olympia?

The winners were given these prizes:

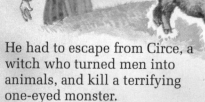

Olive wreath
Palm branches
Ribbons

What is Homer's *Odyssey* about?

The Trojans took the horse into the city to please the gods. However, Greek soldiers were hiding inside. That night, they climbed out, and opened the city gates. The Greeks raided the city and won the war.

9. What was the horse made of?

The *Odyssey* is about Odysseus' adventures on his way home after the Trojan War.

He had to outwit the Sirens who lured sailors to their deaths on the rocks by singing beautifully.

Sirens had the faces of beautiful women, with birds' bodies and clawed feet.

10. Odysseus took:
a) one week;
b) two days;
c) ten years to get home.

He had to escape from Circe, a witch who turned men into animals, and kill a terrifying one-eyed monster.

11. A one-eyed monster is called a:
a) cyclone; b) cyclops; c) cygnet.

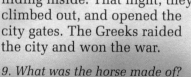

Ancient Rome

Two thousand years ago, Rome was the most important city in Europe. It was the hub of a huge empire which ruled over much of Europe and the Mediterranean lands.

What were Roman baths?

Roman baths were not like modern swimming baths. They had several pools, all at different temperatures. Bathers went from one to another. This left them feeling very clean and refreshed. Men and women went to the baths at different times of day.

1. Unscramble the name of this famous Roman ruler: luiJus Carsae.

A slave working as a hair plucker. It was fashionable to have a smooth, hairless body.

A slave giving a massage.

2. Rome is now the capital of which European country?

Did you know?

To get clean the Romans covered themselves in olive oil, then scraped it off with a scraper, called a *strigilis*. It worked just as well as soap.

3. In some places, people still clean themselves with olive oil. True or false?

4. Some Roman houses had central heating. True or false?

Hot bath

This furnace heated a tank of water. The water was pumped to the hot bath, warm bath and steam room. The furnace was tended by a slave.

Warm bath

What did Romans do for entertainment?

5. Which month is named after Mars, the Roman god of war?

The crowd gave this sign if they wanted the loser to live.

In Rome, fights were put on for the public to watch. These fights were called the Games. The loser was often killed in the fight. If not, the crowd voted whether or not he should be put to death. A brave loser might be allowed to live.

6. Neptune was the Roman god of: a) the moon; b) the wind; c) the sea.

The fighters were criminals or prisoners of war. They might be forced to fight against wild animals, professional fighters or each other.

7. Which of these was a famous fighter who led a revolt against the Roman government: a) Spartacus; b) Diplodocus; c) Muhammad Ali?

8. Professional fighters were called: a) gladiators; b) exterminators; c) mashpotaters.

9. What sign did people give if they wanted the loser to die?

The biggest Games arena in Rome was the Colosseum. It held 48,000 people. This is what it looks like now.

Where were chariot races held?

Chariot races were held in a massive stadium called the Circus Maximus. It held about 280,000 people. Chariot racers belonged to different teams. Supporters in the crowd wore the colors of the team they wanted to win. There were even supporters' clubs to join.

10. The Circus Maximus was larger than any soccer stadium. True or false?

Chariots were very light so that they would go fast.

Most crashes happened on sharp bends.

In the steam room people sweated a lot. This was like a sauna.

Changing room

11. What do you think this hooked knife was for?

The horses' reins were tied around the driver. If the chariot crashed, the driver had to free himself as quickly as possible.

14. The Romans spoke: a) Latin; b) Greek; c) Turkish.

Food seller with sausages and honey cakes.

Where did slaves come from?

Most slaves were prisoners of war that the Roman army captured on their foreign campaigns. They were brought back to Rome to do the worst jobs in return for their keep.

12. Can you see three different jobs that slaves are doing at the baths?

The cold bath (*frigidarium*) was for cooling off after the hot baths or exercise.

13. What is this building?

15. Roman men wore trousers. True or false?

The Vikings

The Vikings came from the far north of Europe. About 1,200 years ago they began exploring the world in search of riches.

Some Vikings raided towns and villages and stole what they wanted. Others traded peacefully in foreign towns.

1. Can you name any of the countries where the Vikings came from?

2. Where did Vikings keep their shields during voyages?

3. What weapon did the Vikings use most often?

What was a Viking raid like?

Vikings tried to catch their victims by surprise. They did not want to waste their energy on a hard fight.

4. How many Vikings have been killed on this raid?

They took prisoners and killed anyone who got in the way. Important prisoners were held for ransom. Poor prisoners were taken back home to be slaves.

Viking ships were flat-bottomed so that they could be sailed into shallow waters. This made surprise attacks easier.

5. Viking boats were called:
a) galleons; b) longships; c) rafts.

Where did Vikings trade?

The Vikings traded mainly with places which they could reach by ship. They founded trading towns all over Europe, such as Dublin in Ireland and Kiev in the Ukraine. Many Vikings settled permanently in trading towns.

9. The name Viking comes from a Viking word meaning: a) King Vic; b) adventurer; c) red beard.

How far did they travel?

Vikings were such good sailors that they even reached North America. They travelled about 7,000 miles (11,000km) there and back. It was 400 years before any other Europeans went there.

10. Which was further away from the Vikings' home, Ireland or North America?

Some traders did not like the Vikings – they thought that the Vikings swore, fought and got drunk too often.

11. In winter, Viking traders made overland journeys on skis. True or false?

Vikings loved Arabian silks and cloths like these.

Treasures from a raid

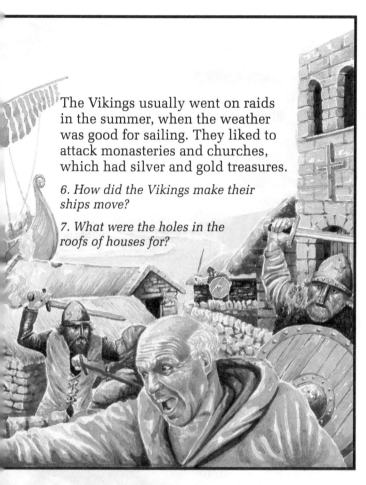

The Vikings usually went on raids in the summer, when the weather was good for sailing. They liked to attack monasteries and churches, which had silver and gold treasures.

6. How did the Vikings make their ships move?

7. What were the holes in the roofs of houses for?

How did the Vikings celebrate?

When they got home, the Vikings held huge feasts that went on for days. Poets called bards told long, exciting stories about famous battles and adventures.

Bard

8. The stories were called: a) sagas; b) lagers; c) lyrics.

Did you know?

Vikings often took their sons with them on trading voyages. That way the boys learned how to be skillful sailors.

Slaves

How were the Vikings buried?

Important warriors were buried or burned in their ships. The Vikings believed that the person's soul sailed to Viking heaven in the ship. There, men fought all day. Every evening there was a huge feast.

12. Viking heaven was called: a) Valhalla; b) Hell; c) Iceland.

Vikings thought that to die of natural causes was boring and cowardly. They called it a "straw death." The best way to die was in battle.

13. Which one of these was not a Viking king: a) Cnut the Great; b) Erik Bloodaxe; c) Herod the Great?

14. Which weekday is named after Thor, the Viking god of thunder?

15. Viking women were called Viqueens. True or false?

43

The Crusades

The Crusades were wars between groups of Christians and Moslems. They began in 1096 and lasted on and off for the next 200 years. The wars were about who should rule Syria and Palestine (see map on the right).

Why was this area important?

Jerusalem in Palestine was a holy place for Moslems. They believed that their leader, Muhammad, rose to heaven from Jerusalem.

1. Why was there a wall around Jerusalem?

Palestine was important to Christians because Jesus Christ had lived there. Christians called the area the Holy Land. They made journeys, called pilgrimages, to pray there.

2. In which town was Jesus Christ born?

ITALY

GREECE

PALESTINE   SYRIA

Jerusalem

Mediterranean Sea

Bethlehem

EGYPT

Moslem soldier

3. This area of water is called: a) the Caribbean Sea; b) the Red Sea; c) the Blue Sea.

Christian soldier

4. What sort of armour is this Christian soldier wearing?

Why did the Crusades begin?

Before the Crusades, Moslems had ruled Palestine for centuries. The Moslems had let Christian pilgrims visit the area safely.

In 1076, though, another Moslem group called the Seljuk Turks took over Palestine. They killed Christians they found there.

In 1096, the Pope, who was head of the Christian Church, asked Christians to take the Holy Land from the Seljuks. He said that if they did, God would forgive all their sins.

About 50,000 people set off from all over Europe. Whole families joined the Crusade, most of them poor. They thought Palestine was a rich land where they would make a good living. This Crusade was called the People's Crusade.

5. Were children allowed to join the Crusades?

The army travelled over 2,000 miles to the Holy Land, mostly on foot.

Who won the People's Crusade?

Many Crusaders starved or died of disease on the way. The Seljuks killed those who got there.

6. 20,000 people died on the way to the Holy Land. True or false?

Did the Christians ever win?

Three years after the start of the People's Crusade, another army of Crusaders captured the Holy Land. It was difficult for them to keep order, though, because most of the people there were Moslems. Bit by bit, the Moslems won the area back.

7. The Moslems had faster horses than the Crusaders. True or false?

Who led the armies?

The Moslem general who won back most of the Holy Land from the Christians was called Saladin. He was a brilliant general and he was fierce but he treated his enemies fairly.

Richard the Lionheart (King Richard I of England) led a Crusade against Saladin. Although he lost the war, Saladin promised to allow pilgrims to visit Jerusalem. Saladin and Richard respected each other although they were enemies.

8. Saladin's sword was called:
a) a scimitar; b) a scythe; c) a scarab.

9. Moslem soldiers were called:
a) Salads; b) Saracens; c) Aladins.

10. Why was Richard I nicknamed "the Lionheart"?

How did the Crusades change Europe?

Crusaders brought back types of food and other goods that were new to Europe. Some of these are shown in the picture.

11. Which of these did the Crusaders NOT bring back to Europe:
a) oranges; b) pepper; c) potatoes?

Moslem castles were very strong so European castle-builders copied them. (See next page.)
▼

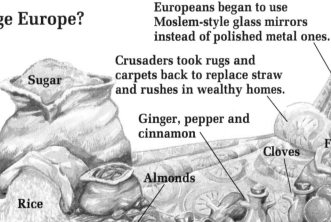

Europeans began to use Moslem-style glass mirrors instead of polished metal ones.

Crusaders took rugs and carpets back to replace straw and rushes in wealthy homes.

Ginger, pepper and cinnamon

Sugar

Rice

Almonds

Cloves

Figs

Dates

Silk

Raisins

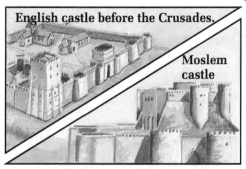

English castle before the Crusades.

Moslem castle

Did you know?

The way numbers are written developed from symbols used by Moslem mathematicians.

12. The numbers on the right were used by Moslem mathematicians. Can you match them to the modern numbers above them?

9 7 4 1

How big was the Moslem Empire?

This map shows how big the Moslem Empire was during the Crusades.

Moslems occupied parts of Spain from the 7th to the 15th century. You can still see Moslem buildings in Spain, such as the Palace of Alhambra in Granada.

14. The Palace of Alhambra was built as a new home for the Pope. True or false?

15. The game below was first played in Europe by Moslems. What is it?

13. The Moslems ruled parts of three continents. True or false?

Syria and Palestine

Spain

Moslem Empire (in red)

Palace of Alhambra

45

A medieval castle

Medieval castles in Europe were the homes of rulers and wealthy landowners. They protected the owner, his subjects and possessions from local bandits or invading armies.

During the 13th century, Crusaders brought back ideas from the Middle East for how to improve European castles. Features marked with a star (★) show some of these ideas.

Where were castles built?

Most castles were built on steep hills or cliffs. This made them difficult to attack. It also gave the defenders a good view of the surrounding area so that they could see approaching enemies.

1. Medieval means: a) dark and eery; b) belonging to the Middle Ages; c) made of stone.

2. Where did the castle defenders get their drinking water from?

Did castles take long to build?

It could take 3,000 builders ten years to build a big castle.

3. Which were stronger – round towers or square ones?

The walls could be up to 16ft (5m) thick.

Turrets made good look-out points.

Well

4. This strong gatehouse is called: a) a barbecue; b) a pelican; c) a barbican.

5. These holes are called: a) murder holes; b) peep holes; c) man holes.

Food stocks

★ The inner wall is higher than the outer wall. This is so that guards on the inner wall can fire down over the outer wall at enemies close by.

If attackers break into the castle, they can be trapped in this passage. Defenders shut the gates and then shoot them through the holes above.

6. What is the name for an underground cell where prisoners were kept?

Castle archers shoot out through these narrow slits, called loops. It is difficult for enemies to shoot back through them.

Notches, called crenels, in the battlements let soldiers lean out to shoot at the enemy.

★ These overhanging wooden shelters are called hourds. They are put up for protection and used like machicolations (see below left).

Shutters give extra protection.

Defenders duck behind merlons to avoid return fire.

★ The picture of the wall is cut away to show a permanent stone overhang with holes in the floor. It is called a machicolation. Soldiers shoot or drop rocks through the holes.

What was a siege?

During a siege, attackers surrounded a castle to stop anyone from entering or leaving it. The people inside could survive for months if they had fresh water and plenty of food stored up.

Attackers hoped that a long siege would cause the people inside to run out of food or get ill. They might just get tired of fighting.

7. The longest siege lasted for six months. True or false?

8. The archers in this picture are using: a) longbows; b) shortbows; c) strongbows.

Did you know?

Once cannons had been invented, castles were no longer so safe. Cannonballs could blast huge holes in the walls. Cannons were invented in the 14th century.

9. The explosive that fired a cannon was: a) dynamite; b) gunpowder.

10. Gunpowder was invented by the Chinese. True or false?

11. Were cannonballs explosive?

What weapons did attackers use?

Attackers used huge catapults, called mangonels and trebuchets. These hurled heavy objects into the castle or at its walls. Sometimes dead and rotting animals were flung into the castle to spread disease.

12. Put these weapons in order of invention: a) mangonel; b) tank; c) spear.

Scaling tower

Mangonel

Trebuchets

13. What is this type of bridge called?

14. What is this siege weapon called?

15. What is this deep channel of water called?

The Aztecs and the Incas

About 500 years ago, much of Central and South America was ruled by two powerful tribes, the Aztecs and the Incas. They worshipped the sun and had so much gold that they even used it to decorate gardens. Less than 50 years later, though, their empires had disappeared. They had been destroyed by Spanish conquerors who came in search of fabulous wealth.

Tenochtitlan

Aztec Empire

Cuzco

1. Which mountain range ran through the Inca Empire: a) Alps; b) Andes; c) Himalayas?

Inca Empire

Who were the Aztecs?

The Aztecs ruled several other tribes in part of what is now Mexico. Their king was called the Great Speaker. He had a deputy called Snake Woman. These two people stood for the man and woman who had created the earth.

2. The Spanish invaders were called: a) bandits; b) cowboys; c) conquistadores.

Did you know?

The post of Snake Woman was always held by a man. This was because only men were allowed to rule in the Aztec kingdom.

3. The South Americans sometimes ate guinea pigs. True or false?

What did Aztecs wear?

The more important someone was, the grander the clothes they were allowed to wear. It was illegal for a lowly person to copy a powerful person's clothing.

What was the Aztec capital city?

The Aztec capital was called Tenochtitlan. It was built on an island in the middle of a lake. It had a main square with temples and palaces around it.

4. The capital of present-day Mexico is called: a) Tenochtitlan; b) Mexico City; c) Los Angeles.

The Great Temple

Warrior

5. Which of these people did the Aztecs think was the most important: a) warrior; b) farmer; c) weaver?

Where was the Inca kingdom?

The Inca kingdom ran down the west of South America. It was larger than the Aztec Empire. The Inca king, Sapa Inca, lived in Cuzco, the capital city. Most people in the Inca kingdom were farmers or craftspeople.

How did the Incas travel?

Incas travelled on foot. A huge network of tracks criss-crossed the Empire. There were huts, called rest houses, a day's walk apart so that travellers had somewhere to spend the night.

12. Incas made clothing out of horsehair. True or false?

Rest house

Bridge made from thick rope.

Runners carried messages from town to town.

Steps were built up steep hills.

There were no horses in America. Incas used these animals to carry heavy loads, instead.

11. What is this animal?

Who did the Aztecs worship?

Aztecs had thousands of gods, from a flower god to a war god. The Aztecs believed that the gods could bring them good or bad luck. They tried to keep the gods happy by giving them gifts.

What happened in the Great Temple?

The Aztecs worshipped their gods in the Great Temple. Often they made a human sacrifice, that is, they killed someone as an offering to a god. Every evening they made a human sacrifice to the sun god. They hoped this would mean the sun would rise again the next morning.

6. Aztecs made purple dye out of sea snail slime. True or false?

8. Which Aztec god is this?

Weaver

Farmer

Cocoa beans

7. Which is worth more, the bird or the rug?

What happened in the market?

In the market in the main square, Aztecs swapped one sort of goods for another. They used cocoa beans as small change if one half of the swap was worth more that the other.

9. Swapping goods instead of selling them is called: a) bartering; b) bantering; c) battering.

10. This bird is: a) a toucan; b) an albatross; c) a turkey.

Why did the empires collapse?

Spanish invaders first reached Central and South America early in the 16th century. They had several important advantages over the Aztecs and Incas, as shown below.

Aztecs and Incas had not seen horses before.

Aztecs and Incas always travelled on foot. The Spaniards had horses, so they could travel much faster along the Inca tracks.

13. How did the Spaniards travel to South America?

Aztec and Inca warriors

The Spaniards had guns. Aztecs and Incas only had arrows, knives, spears and clubs.

Spanish weapons

Aztec and Inca weapons

The Aztecs and Incas had no resistance to European diseases brought by the Spaniards.

14. Thousands of Aztecs and Incas died from catching colds. True or false?

Who took over South America?

The Spanish conquerors were the first Europeans to explore South America. Some set up their own kingdoms. Many boundaries of present-day South American countries can be traced back to these Spanish kingdoms.

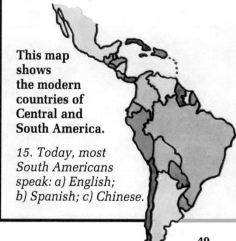

This map shows the modern countries of Central and South America.

15. Today, most South Americans speak: a) English; b) Spanish; c) Chinese.

Inventions and discoveries

People don't always welcome new inventions and discoveries. Here are some important or useful ones which were unpopular at first.

When did people disagree about trousers?

An American called Amelia Bloomer designed trousers for women in 1853.

In those days, smartly dressed women had to wear bulky dresses. Many people thought that trousers should only be worn by men. It was a hundred years before trousers for women became fashionable.

1. What were the trousers designed by Amelia Bloomer called?

2. What type of hat is the man wearing?

This is what Amelia Bloomer's trousers looked like.

Who was imprisoned for a discovery?

In the 1630s, Galileo, an Italian scientist, wrote a book supporting the discovery that the earth and the other planets travel around the sun.

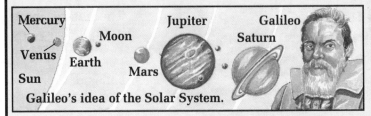

Mercury
Venus
Sun
Moon
Earth
Mars
Jupiter
Galileo
Saturn

Galileo's idea of the Solar System.

This made the leaders of the Catholic Church angry. They believed that the earth was the middle of the universe and that the sun and other planets went around the earth.

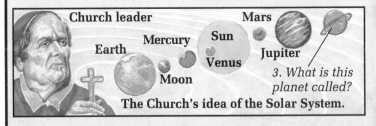

Church leader
Earth
Mercury
Moon
Sun
Venus
Jupiter
Mars

3. What is this planet called?

The Church's idea of the Solar System.

Galileo was accused of lying and put on trial. He was forced to plead guilty and was imprisoned in his own home.

4. Was Galileo right or wrong?

5. What are scientists who study the stars called?

Why did steam engines cause riots?

Steam-powered machinery was first used on farms and in factories in the early 19th century. Each machine did the job of several workers, so many lost their jobs. This led to riots. Usually the rioters attacked the steam engine, as shown here.

6. Can you think of another way steam engines were used, apart from on farms and in factories?

7. The invention of steam engines led to a period of great change called: a) the Industrial Revolution; b) the Reformation; c) the Iron Age.

TV pictures are made up of rows of dots. Modern TVs have over 600 rows.

Radio

Did you know?

People saw the first TV broadcast via their radios. The radios were fitted with a device to pick up the TV signals. Only a few people saw the first pictures. They showed a person sitting down.

8. Which came first, cinema or television?

9. The first regular TV broadcasts were made in: a) 1336; b) 1936; c) 1986.

What is this cartoon about?

The cartoon above made fun of a doctor called Edward Jenner, in 1802. He had found a way to prevent people from catching a deadly disease called smallpox. He injected patients with germs from a similar but non-deadly disease called cowpox. People who had been injected did not catch smallpox.

People found this discovery, called inoculation, hard to believe. Nowadays, though, inoculation is used to prevent hundreds of different diseases.

10. Another word for inoculation is:
a) incubation; b) vaccination; c) transfusion.

11. Dairymaids often caught cowpox. True or false?

12. Which of these illnesses cannot be prevented by inoculation: a) flu; b) measles; c) a cold?

Why was Charles Darwin unpopular?

About 130 years ago, the scientist Charles Darwin made himself unpopular because he disagreed with a story from the Bible. The story told how God created the earth and everything on it in six days.

Darwin said that over thousands of years the earth's environment changes. Animals and plants have to adapt to survive. Some die out but those that adapt become more efficient. Darwin gave many examples of this process. (See pages 34-35).

13. Darwin's theory is called:
a) revolution; b) evolution; c) evaluation.

Powerful beak to crush seeds and nuts. ▼

▲ **Sharp, strong beak to dig into cacti and chew seeds.**

▲ **Thin beak to probe for insects and pierce fruit.**

One of Darwin's examples came from a study of birds on an island in the Pacific Ocean. He found that similar birds had developed different beaks to eat various types of food.

14. These birds are all types of: a) finch;
b) parrot; c) ostrich.

Why was nuclear power unpopular?

Nuclear fuel was first used in power stations in the 1950s. If the fuel leaks, it poisons everything that it touches, even the air. Many people were worried about this and went on demonstrations to protest against nuclear power.

Until the 1950s, most power stations ran on oil or coal. These are safer to use than nuclear fuel but the supply may run out eventually. Also, the smoke from them dissolves in the rain. When the rain falls it damages pastures and forests. This sort of rain is called acid rain.

In 1986, nuclear fuel leaked from a power station at Chernobyl in the Ukraine. The environment for several miles around was ruined. It is still not safe for people to live near Chernobyl, eat food grown there or drink water from the region.

15. Put the following in order of invention:
a) nuclear power; b) steam power; c) electricity.

The red area shows how far the wind blew the nuclear pollution. Scientists had to check that the areas were safe for people and animals.

Great Britain

Scandinavia

France

Germany

Eastern Europe

Chernobyl

Ukraine

Italy

The Wild West

There used to be hundreds of American Indian tribes in North America. As European settlers arrived, they began to take over Indian land. By the 19th century, much of the land was being used for huge cattle farms, worked on by cowboys.

1. What were the Indians' tents called?

2. What were the tents made from?

3. What is an American Indian woman called?

Tomahawk

Where do American Indians live now?

Some Indians still try to live their traditional way of life in areas set aside for them, called reservations. The rest live like other Americans.

4. For good luck in battle, Indians danced:
a) a deathdance;
b) a wardance;
c) a tango.

5. American Indians wore shoes made from buffalo leather called:
a) jerkins;
b) bodkins;
c) moccasins.

How did the Indians live?

Many tribes trailed herds of buffalo all over the prairies. When hunting, Indians often wore the skins of other animals. This disguised them and their scent from the prey.

What did cowboys do?

Cowboys worked on huge cattle farms, called ranches. The biggest cattle herds had over 15,000 cattle. Cowboys used horses to get around the ranches to check the cattle. The horse usually belonged to the ranch owner but the cowboy owned his own saddle. Cowboys spent most of their working life in the saddle.

6. These cattle are:
a) blackhorn cattle;
b) shorthorn cattle;
c) longhorn cattle.

Why did Indians and cowboys fight?

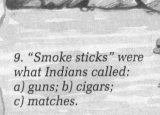

Ranch owners took over land where Indians had lived for centuries. Sometimes, cowboys used force to push the Indians and the buffalo which they hunted off the ranches. The Indians might attack the ranches in revenge.

9. "Smoke sticks" were what Indians called:
a) guns; b) cigars;
c) matches.

Did you know?

The feathers and warpaint that Indians wore had special meanings.

These feathers meant he had been wounded in battle.

This paint meant he would chase intruders away.

India

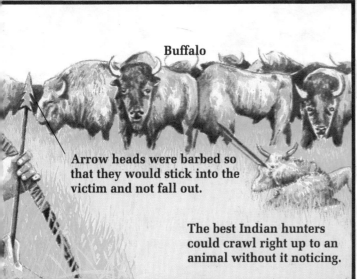

Buffalo

Arrow heads were barbed so that they would stick into the victim and not fall out.

The best Indian hunters could crawl right up to an animal without it noticing.

Who were the cowboys?

Most cowboys were young, unmarried men. They usually slept in dormitories at the ranch. Ten good cowboys could manage a herd of 1,000 cattle.

12. Most cowboys wore hats called: a) stetsons; b) top hats; c) bowlers.

13. Why did cowboys' hats have wide brims?

Bandana

7. American Indians had no horses before European settlers brought horses to America. True or False?

8. What is this called?

Winchester rifle

Six-shooter

14. Why was the pistol called a six-shooter?

Leather leggings, called chaps, protected trousers and legs from brush and barbed wire.

Why were they called "Red Indians"?

The explorer Christopher Columbus named the American Indians "Red Indians." 500 years ago, he sailed from Spain to find a sea route to India. Instead, he landed in America. He thought the people he met were Indians, but with skin a redder shade of brown.

North America

Spain

South America

Brand for marking cattle.

10. Which of these is the odd one out: a) Sioux; b) Apache; c) Zulu?

11. Which two of these countries now make up North America: USA, Peru, Canada, Brazil, Chile?

15. Why were cattle branded?

Spur

53

Trains, cars and planes

Before the invention of trains, cars and planes, a journey that now takes hours could take days or even weeks.

People travelled overland either on foot, on horseback or in horsedrawn carriages. Roads were dirt tracks. When they were dry they were hard and bumpy. When they were wet they became deep, sticky bogs.

1. How many different forms of transportation can you see on these two pages?

When did the first passenger train run?

The first passenger train service was in Kent in southern England. It opened in 1830 with a journey only 1 mile (1.6km) long. A steam engine, called *Invicta*, pulled the train at about 12mph (20kmph).

2. The first trains were slower than a galloping horse. True or false?

Most carriages had no roofs.

Invicta

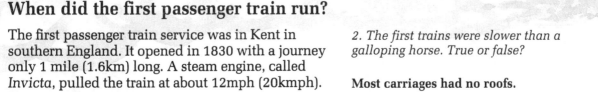

Did you know?

The longest railway line is over 5,600 miles (9,000km) long. It was built between 1891 and 1905 and stretched from the west to the east of the Russian Empire.

3. Does the Russian Empire still exist?

4. The longest railway is called: a) the Great Western Railway; b) the Trans-Siberian Railway; c) the Orient Express.

By 1916 there were over 250,000 miles (400,000 km) of railway in the USA.

RUSSIAN EMPIRE
Moscow
Nakhodka
CHINA

What was the first car like?

Early cars still looked similar to horse carriages. Karl Benz made the first car in Germany just over 100 years ago. A fuel engine drove the back wheels. Its top speed was 10mph (16kmph).

5. Can you name a modern car company that uses Benz's name?

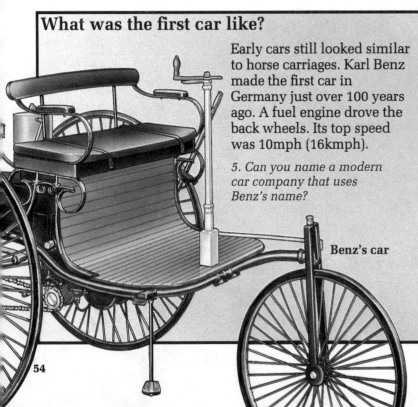

Benz's car

Were cars popular?

At first most people hated cars. They said they were dirty, noisy and a danger to horses and people. For many years after the car's invention only rich people could afford them.

Early car

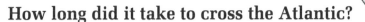

How long did it take to cross the Atlantic?

Before air travel, a journey between America and Europe took almost a week on the fastest ship. It can now take just three and a quarter hours by jet.

12. Which came first: a) canoe; b) car; c) bicycle?

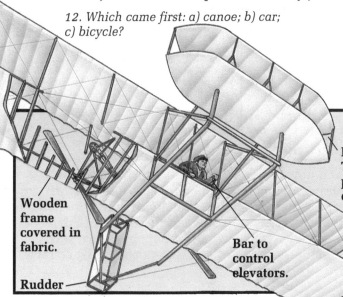

Wooden frame covered in fabric.

Rudder

Elevators. These made the plane go up or down.

Bar to control elevators.

Orville Wright's plane

The Montgolfier brothers' balloon

Who were the first people to fly?

The Montgolfier brothers made a balloon flight in Paris about 200 years ago. The balloon was filled with hot air to make it rise.

Who flew the first plane?

Orville Wright made the first flight in a powered plane in 1903. He flew for 12 seconds and rose about 10ft (3m) into the air.

13. The wings of Wright's plane flapped like a bird's. True or false?

When were the first passenger flights?

The first passenger air service began in 1910 in Germany. It used airships called Zeppelins. They were filled with a gas that was lighter than air to make them float.

14. No airships ever crashed. True or false?

Zeppelin

Rudders to steer from side to side.

Moveable engines for steering.

Gas was held in bags, called cells.

Walkway for workers.

Workers could climb outside to fix holes while the ship was in flight.

Metal frame

Fabric skin

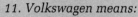

15. A Zeppelin could carry 5,000 passengers. True or false?

Gondola. Passengers and flight crew travelled in here.

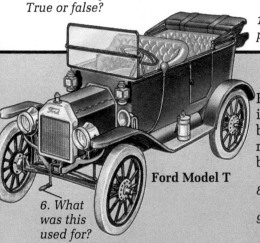

Ford Model T

6. What was this used for?

Henry Ford's company made the first car that ordinary people could afford in 1908. It was called the Model T and Ford made 16 million of them altogether.

7. For many years the Ford Model T was only available in: a) pink; b) black; c) silver.

Ford stopped making the Model T in 1927 but it remained the world's best-selling car until the 1960s. The record was broken by a car made by Volkswagen, shown on the right.

8. What type of Volkswagen is it?

9. Where is its engine?

Early cars had solid rubber tires. Modern tires are filled with air for a softer ride and better grip on the road.

10. Air-filled tires are called: a) pneumatic; b) rheumatic; c) aromatic.

11. Volkswagen means: a) people's car; b) little bug; c) road machine.

The twentieth century

There have probably been more changes since 1900 than during any other century. On these pages you can read about some of the events which have taken place this century.

What was the Russian Revolution about?

Lenin, the Bolshevik leader, speaking to factory workers.

A factory run by the new government.

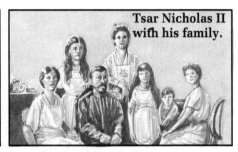

Tsar Nicholas II with his family.

Before the Revolution, the emperor of Russia, called the tsar, chose the government from among his noblemen and those he preferred. The leaders of the Revolution, called the Bolsheviks, wanted a government made up of ordinary people. They thought this would be better for most Russians.

The Bolsheviks seized power in 1917. The new government owned and ran every business in the country. They thought that this would benefit everyone. The system was called communism.

1. What did the Bolshevik flag look like?

In 1918, Tsar Nicholas II was shot by Bolshevik supporters. In 1923, the Russian Empire became known as the Union of Soviet Socialist Republics, or USSR. It was the first communist country.

2. The USSR never had a tsar after 1918. True or false?

Who were the Nazis?

The Nazis were a German political party. They governed Germany from 1933 to 1945. They rose to power because they promised to make Germany strong again after years of hardship following World War I.

The man in the photograph (left) was the leader of the Nazi party.

3. What was his name?

4. Was the Nazi symbol: a) a fox; b) a swastika; c) a star?

How did World War II begin?

During the late 1930s, the Nazis began to take over parts of Europe. In 1939, Britain and France declared war on Germany to try to stop them.

Germany continued to invade other countries. In 1941, the USA and USSR joined Britain and France. In 1945, Germany surrendered.

Denmark Norway
Holland
Belgium

Countries invaded by Germany before World War II.

Countries invaded by Germany in the first year of World War II.

5. Did Germany invade Great Britain?

Great Britain

Germany

France

Poland: invaded in 1939, provoking declaration of war.

Czechoslovakia: invaded in 1938.

Austria: taken over in 1938.

The German army invaded Holland in 1940.

6. Countries that join forces in war are called: a) chums; b) allies; c) troops.

7. How long did World War II last?

Did you know?

The first nuclear weapon was used during World War II. It was a bomb dropped by the USA on Hiroshima in Japan in 1945. Japan was on Germany's side in World War II.

Hiroshima after the bomb.

8. There have been: a) two; b) five; c) 23 World Wars.

What was the Cultural Revolution?

Communists took power in China in 1949, after fighting the old government for over 20 years. By the mid-1960s, they felt that people were forgetting the true aims of communism. They started a scheme which was supposed to increase support for Chinese communism. It was called the Cultural Revolution.

The government banned plays and books that supported life before communism. New books and plays had to praise Chinese communism or say that life had been unfair before it.

9. A war between people of the same country is called: a) a star war; b) a civil war; c) a cold war.

Leaders of the Cultural Revolution sent gangs of young people around China to smash up reminders of the old way of life. The gangs, called the Red Guards, also attacked people who opposed communism.

10. Which was the first country to have a communist government?

An inspector sacks a teacher who criticized communism.

In schools, teachers had to praise Chinese communism to their pupils.

This is a play in support of communism being performed during the Cultural Revolution.

Red Guards burning books about life before communism.

The Red Guards killed thousands of people. They were finally banned in 1969.

When were computers invented?

The first computer was built during World War II. It was designed to crack secret codes used by the German and Japanese armies.

During the 1950s and 1960s, scientists invented smaller and smaller components until thousands could be fitted into a space the size of a fingernail.

Components are held inside here on a slice of glass-like material called silicon.

11. This is called: a) a bug; b) a byte; c) a chip.

The first computer filled a large room because its electronic parts, called components, were so big.

12. Silicon is mined from Silicon Valley, California. True or false?

Who made the first space flight?

The first space flight was made by Yuri Gagarin (USSR) in 1962. His flight lasted less than two hours.

Gagarin's spaceship went around the earth once.

In 1969, people landed on the moon for the first time.

13. Which country did the first people on the moon come from?

What were the colonies?

In the first half of the 20th century, most of Africa and India were governed by European countries. The Europeans often took the best land and products for themselves. The countries they ruled were called colonies. People in the colonies wanted to govern themselves. Some colonies had to fight their rulers before they won their independence.

14. Which of these is not an African country: a) Nigeria; b) Argentina; c) Kenya?

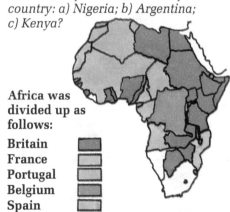

Africa was divided up as follows:

Britain
France
Portugal
Belgium
Spain

Algeria fought its rulers for eight years before it won independence, in 1962.

15. Which country ruled Algeria before it won independence?

Djibouti was the last African country to gain independence, in 1977.

History Megaquiz

Try these quizzes to see how much you can remember from the rest of Part Two. Write your answers down and then check on page 64 to see how many you got right.

Famous people

Match the descriptions of these ten famous people with their names, listed in the blue box below.

1. A scientist who developed the theory of evolution.
2. An Ancient Egyptian king who died at age 18.
3. A leader of the Moslem army during the Crusades.
4. The title given to the Aztec king.
5. The inventor of the first fuel-driven car.
6. The first person to fly a powered plane.
7. The leader of Germany in the 1930s and 1940s.
8. The scientist who was imprisoned for writing that the earth travels around the sun.
9. The last tsar of Russia.
10. The hero of Homer's epic poem, the *Odyssey*.

a) Adolf Hitler	c) Galileo	e) Nicholas II	g) Great Speaker	i) Karl Benz
b) Orville Wright	d) Odysseus	f) Tutankhamen	h) Saladin	j) Charles Darwin

Clothes and fashions

Who wore these costumes and hairstyles?

True or false?

1. The Ancient Romans used soap to get clean.
2. Viking warriors were buried or burned in ships.
3. Cowboys rode bicycles around cattle farms.
4. The first computer was smaller than this book.
5. The women's parts in Greek plays were played by men.
6. Dr. Edward Jenner found a way to stop people from catching smallpox.
7. The car that the Ford Motor Company first sold in 1908 was called the Model X.
8. During a siege, castle dwellers were allowed out to fetch food and water.
9. Tenochtitlan, the Aztec capital, was built in the middle of a lake.
10. At the Greek sports festival in Olympia, winners received gold medals.

Which came first?

Can you put each set of three people, animals or things in order of appearance or invention?

1. Tyrannosaurus rex; Stegosaurus; jellyfish.
2. Viking; *conquistador*; Bolshevik.
3. Computer; steam engine; horse and cart.
4. Cannon: sword; six-shooter.
5. Tsar Nicholas II; Richard I; Tutankhamen.
6. Inoculation; television; water well.
7. Model T Ford; Viking longship; chariot.
8. Pyramid; Palace of Alhambra; nuclear power station.
9. Amelia Bloomer; Homer; Lenin.
10. USSR; Roman Empire; Inca Empire.

Close-ups

These are all close-ups of parts of pictures in Part Two. Can you recognize what they show?

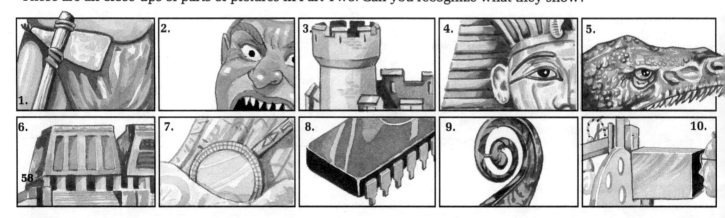

Where in the world?

Can you match the places marked on the map with the descriptions below?

1. Christopher Columbus was trying to sail to this country when he landed in America.
2. The Cultural Revolution took place in this country.
3. There was a nuclear accident here in 1986.
4. *Conquistadores* came from this country.
5. There are hieroglyphics in the tombs here.
6. The Aztecs used to live here.
7. A famous sports festival was held in this city.
8. The Circus Maximus was in this city.
9. The scientist Galileo lived in this country.
10. This country had the first passenger train service.

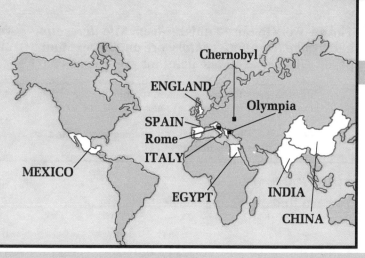

The time line

Can you match these events with the dates on the time line below?

1. Modern man first appears.
2. Homer the poet makes up the *Iliad*.
3. Spanish *conquistadores* attack the Aztecs.
4. Dinosaurs dominate the earth.
5. Egyptians start building pyramids.
6. Rome is the most powerful city in Europe.
7. Vikings begin exploring the world.
8. The People's Crusade begins.
9. Cannons are invented.
10. The first people land on the moon.

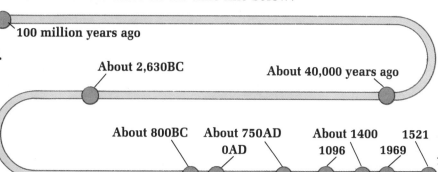

100 million years ago

About 2,630BC

About 40,000 years ago

About 800BC   About 750AD   About 1400   1521
0AD   1096   1969

What do you know?

1. Most Ancient Egyptians were not buried in pyramids. Where were they buried?
2. What lived on earth until 65 million years ago?
3. Can you name a group of people who were not allowed to vote in Ancient Athens?
4. What was the name given to Viking storytellers?
5. Which company made the best-selling car ever?
6. Tsar is a Russian word. What does it mean?
7. What weapon gave European invaders a big advantage over the Aztecs and Incas?
8. Were the first TV pictures in color or black-and-white?
9. Where might you find a loop, a crenel and a merlon?
10. When hunting, what did American Indians often wear to disguise themselves?

Silhouettes

All these silhouettes are of things that appear in Part Two. How many can you recognize?

      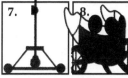

What else do you know?

1. Which was the biggest dinosaur?
2. What country did the first man in space come from?
3. Besides comedies, what sort of plays could you watch in a Greek theatre?
4. What was in the Montgolfier brothers' balloon to make it rise?
5. On the tracks which crossed the Inca Empire, how long did it usually take travellers to walk from one rest house to another?
6. What did the Ancient Romans watch at the Colosseum?
7. What new type of fuel was used in power stations in the 1950s?
8. Did the Ancient Romans know how to make hot water?
9. Who led the Christian army against Saladin during the Crusades?
10. What was the name given to the huge cattle farms where cowboys worked?

Quiz answers

The answers to the 12 quizzes from *The dinosaur age* to *The twentieth century* are on the next four pages. Give yourself one point for every answer you get right. The chart below helps you to find out how well you have done in each quiz.

0-5	Read through the answers, then try the quiz again. See how many answers you can remember second time around.
6-10	Quite good. Think carefully about the questions and you might get more answers right.

11-14	Good score. If you get this score on most of the quizzes, you can be very pleased with yourself.
15	Excellent. If you do this well in more than half the quizzes, you are a history genius!

Your score overall

You can find out your average score over all 12 quizzes like this:

1. Add up your scores on all 12 quizzes.
2. Divide this total by 12. This is your average score. How well did you do?

General knowledge

All the answers to general knowledge questions are marked ★. These questions are probably the hardest in the quizzes. Add up how many of them you got right across all 12 quizzes. There are 50 of them in total. If you got over 30 right, your general knowledge is good.

The dinosaur age

1. a) Dinosaur means "terrible lizard."
2. The name Tyrannosaurus rex means "Tyrant Lizard King."
3. Stegosaurus used its tail as a weapon.
4. True. Dinosaurs laid tough, leathery eggs in the sand.
5. b) Bones preserved in rock are called fossils.
6. False. Brachiosarurus was too big to climb trees.
7. True. No one knows what color dinosaurs were as no skins remain.
★ 8. c) A hippopotamus is a mammal.
9. b) Animal life evolved from bacteria in the sea.
10. No. No dinosaurs could fly. However, flying reptiles such as pterodactyls lived during the dinosaur age.

Pterodactyl

★11. Eight of the animals still exist. They are: crocodile, frog, snake, tortoise, ape, human, jellyfish and shrew. Only score a point if you spotted them all. If you spotted the shrew but did not get its name right, score a point anyway, since it is difficult to identify.
★12. a) A meat-eater is a carnivore. A herbivore eats plants. Animals that eat meat and plants are omnivores.
13. No. The biggest dinosaur found so far is Brachiosaurus. These pictures show how big it was compared to T. rex.

14. c) About 800 different kinds of dinosaur have been found so far.
15. None. Man did not exist.

Ancient Egypt

★ 1. There is still a country called Egypt. It has been called Egypt for nearly 5,000 years.

2. False. All the ancient pyramids still exist, although poorly built ones have partly collapsed.
3. Anubis was a type of dog called a jackal. (Score a point if you guessed dog.)
4. b) Embalmed bodies are known as mummies.
5. True. You can see mummies in some history museums.
6. c) Elizabeth I was not a queen of Egypt. She was Queen of England from 1558 to 1603.
7. The pointed capstone went at the top of the pyramid.
8. b) A sphynx has a lion's body.
9. The pyramids were covered with white limestone (see page 36).
★10. Egyptian kings were called pharaohs.

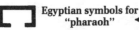
Egyptian symbols for "pharaoh"

★11. No. Tutankhamen's tomb was cut into the rock. When Tutankhamen reigned, the pyramids were already historic monuments over 1,200 years old.
12. Egyptian children did not usually wear any clothes at all during the summer (see picture on page 37).
★13. Cairo. This is the capital city of Egypt.
★14. c) The symbols on the wall were called hieroglyphics.
15. The symbol on the right means "to walk."

Ancient Greece

★ 1. Athens is the present capital of Greece (see map below).
2. On page 38, the mask on the left shows happiness and the other mask shows anger. (Score a point if you guessed other similar feelings.)

Mask of a tragic heroine

3. Yes. Translations of some Ancient Greek plays are still performed.
4. False. The Greeks built open-air theatres in hillside hollows so that actors' voices would be heard right at the back.
5. b) Democracy means "governed by the people."
6. True. Olives were valuable. They were crushed to make olive oil, which was sold to foreign traders.
7. a) Homer's poems were called epics.
★ 8. Greece is part of Europe.
★ 9. The model horse was made of wood.
10. c) Odysseus took ten years to return home to Troy. This map shows where Troy probably was.

11. b) Another name for a one-eyed monster is a cyclops.
12. From left to right the gods are: a) Poseidon; d) Athene; b) Aphrodite; c) Zeus.
13. True. This is one luxury that the Spartans allowed themselves.
14. From left to right the sports are: discus throwing, wrestling, relay racing, javelin throwing.
15. The Olympic Games are named after the sports festival at Olympia.

Ancient Rome

★ 1. Julius Caesar. He ruled Rome from 49BC until 44BC, when he was murdered by his rivals.

★ 2. Rome is now the capital of Italy (see map below).

The Roman Empire is shaded in grey.

GREECE
Rome
ITALY

3. True. In some hot countries where there is not much water, people use olive oil to clean themselves.

4. True. Wealthy Romans had a form of central heating called a hypocaust in their homes. Hot air flowed under the floors and up the walls through channels built of hollow tiles.

5. The month of March is named after the Roman god Mars.

★ 6. c) Neptune was the Roman god of the sea.

7. a) Spartacus was a professional fighter who organized a revolt against the Roman government in 73BC. He was defeated in 71BC.

8. a) The fighters were called gladiators.

9. If spectators wanted a fighter to die, they gave a thumbs-down sign. If they wanted a fighter to live, they gave a thumbs-up sign.

Live   Die

10. True. The largest soccer stadium in the world, the Maracana Stadium in Brazil, holds 205,000 people.

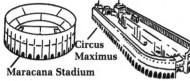

Maracana Stadium   Circus Maximus

11. The driver used his knife to cut himself free if there was a crash.

12. At the baths, there are slaves giving a massage, plucking hair and tending the furnace. (Only score a point if you noticed all three.)

13. The building is the toilet block.

★14. a) The Ancient Romans spoke Latin.

15. False. Roman men wore tunics or togas. Togas were for formal wear. They were very heavy. Tunics were much lighter and more comfortable. Togas were made out of a piece of cloth 15ft (5m) in diameter.

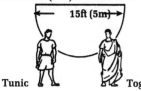

15ft (5m)

Tunic   Toga

The Vikings

★ 1. The Vikings came from the lands which are now the countries Denmark, Norway and Sweden. This area is now called Scandinavia. Score a point if you got any of these.

Sweden
Norway
Denmark

2. Vikings fastened their shields to the sides of their ships during voyages (see picture on page 43).

3. Vikings used swords most often. They even gave their swords names, such as Fierce One and Leg Biter.

Viking sword

4. One Viking has been killed.

5. b) Viking boats were called longships.

6. Vikings could make their ships move in two ways. When it was windy they used a sail. When it was calm they rowed the ship. Score a point if you got either of these.

Sail for windy weather.   Oars used in calm weather.

★ 7. The hole in the roof let smoke from a fire inside the house escape.

8. a) Viking stories were called sagas. A saga might last as long as a feature film does today.

9. b) The name Viking comes from the Viking word for adventurer.

★10. North America was further from the Vikings' home than Ireland.

11. True. The Vikings used skis and skates made of smoothed bone for winter trading journeys.

Viking skate

12. a) Viking heaven was called Valhalla. It meant "palace of the killed."

13. c) Herod the Great was a ruler of Palestine who died in 4BC.

14. Thursday is named after Thor, the Viking god of thunder. The other weekdays are named after the following:

Sunday: the Sun
Monday: the Moon
Tuesday: Tyr, Viking god of law
Wednesday: Odin, Viking god of war
Friday: Frigg, Viking goddess of love
Saturday: Saturn, Roman god of farming

15. False. There is no special name for Viking women.

The Crusades

1. The wall around Jerusalem was there to protect the city. (Score a point if you got the general idea.)

★ 2. Jesus Christ was born in Bethlehem.

★ 3. b) This area of water is called the Red Sea.

★ 4. This soldier is wearing a type of meshed metal armor called chain mail.

5. Yes, whole families joined the Crusades. One Crusade, called the Children's Crusade, which set off in 1212, consisted of thousands of children. Most starved to death or were sold as slaves before they reached Palestine.

6. True. Most of the People's Crusaders died from disease or lack of food.

7. True. Moslems rode small Arab horses that could dart around the battlefield. The Crusaders' horses were heavier and slower. They had to carry a knight in full armor.

Arab horse   Crusader's horse

8. a) Saladin's sword was called a scimitar. The Crusaders' swords, called broadswords, were heavier.

Scimitar   Broadsword

9. b) Moslem soldiers were called Saracens.

★10. Richard I was called "the Lionheart" because of his courage. Lions are supposed to be brave animals.

11. c) The Crusaders did not take potatoes back to Europe. These were first taken to Europe from America about 300 years after the Crusades.

12. The numbers as they appear from left to right are 1,4,7 and 9. Here is the whole set of numbers used by Moslem mathematicians, from 0 to 9.

0 1 2 3 4 5 6 7 8 9

13. True. The Moslems ruled lands in Africa, Asia and Europe.

14. False. The Palace of Alhambra was built for Granada's Moslem kings.

★15. The game is chess. The Moslems learned chess when they invaded India in the 11th and 12th centuries. It became popular all over the Moslem Empire.

Moslem chess pieces

King   Knight

A medieval castle

1. b) Medieval means belonging to the Middle Ages. This period lasted from the 5th to the 15th century.
2. The defenders got drinking water from a well. Its position in the picture on page 46 is shown here.

Well

3. Round towers were stronger than square ones because rocks glanced off their surface and did less damage.
4. c) The fortified gatehouse is called a barbican.
5. a) The holes are called murder holes. If attackers went under the murder holes, the defenders fired at them through the holes or poured boiling liquid down onto them.
★ 6. An underground cell for prisoners is called a dungeon.
7. False. Some castle sieges lasted up to a year. A besieged city could last even longer. For example, the siege of Acre in Palestine in 1189 lasted for two years.
8. a) The archers are using longbows.

A longbow was as long as the archer was tall.

9. b) The explosive that fired a cannon was gunpowder. Dynamite was not invented until 1865.
10. True. The Chinese invented gunpowder about 1,200 years ago.
11. No, cannonballs did not explode.
★ 12. The order of invention is: c) spear, a) mangonel, b) tank. Spears have been used for thousands of years. An early type of mangonel was built by the Ancient Greeks. Tanks were first used in 1916, during World War I.
★ 13. This type of bridge is called a drawbridge. It could be drawn up to make the castle harder to reach.

Drawbridge down   Drawbridge up

★ 14. The weapon is called a battering ram. The attackers used it to break down the castle gates.
★ 15. The channel of water is called a moat. Early castles were often built on a man-made mound of earth. The earth was dug from a circular trench that was usually filled with water to make a moat.

The Aztecs and the Incas

★ 1. b) The Andes ran through the Inca Empire. The Alps are in Europe and the Himalayas are in Asia.
2. c) The Spanish invaders were called *conquistadores*, which is the Spanish word for "conquerors."
3. True. Incas bred guinea pigs to eat during religious festivals.
4. b) The capital of Mexico is Mexico City. It is the world's biggest city. Part of it covers the site of the old city of Tenochtitlan.

This Aztec building was found when a railway tunnel was dug in Mexico city.

5. a) The Aztecs thought the warrior was the most important. You can tell this because his clothes are finer than the farmer's or the weaver's.
6. True. They also made a red dye, called cochineal, out of beetles, and green dye out of tree bark.
7. The rug is worth more than the bird. This is why the bird-seller is offering cocoa beans as part of the deal.
8. The picture shows the Aztec god of war. He is carrying weapons.
9. a) Swapping goods instead of selling them is called bartering. The picture below shows some examples of what cocoa beans were worth.

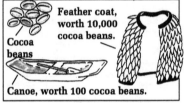
Cocoa beans
Feather coat, worth 10,000 cocoa beans.
Canoe, worth 100 cocoa beans.

10. c) The bird is a turkey. Until the 1500s, turkeys were only found in America. They were taken to Europe by the Spanish.
★ 11. It is a llama. Llamas came from the area now called Peru.

Peru
SOUTH AMERICA
Inca llama brooch

12. False. There were no horses in America until they were brought by the Spaniards.
13. The Spaniards sailed to South America. They crossd the Atlantic Ocean in ships called galleons.
14. True. Colds and other European illnesses such as measles were deadly to the Aztecs and Incas.
15. b) Today, most South Americans speak Spanish.

Inventions and discoveries

1. The trousers were called bloomers, after Amelia Bloomer.
★ 2. The man is wearing a top hat.
3. Saturn. (It is labelled in the picture above on page 50.)
★ 4. Galileo was right. Galileo developed the telescope, with which he was able to watch the planets.

Galileo was the first to see the planet Saturn, in 1610.

Galileo's telescope

5. Scientists who study stars and planets are called astronomers.
★ 6. Steam engines pulled trains and powered ships and early types of cars. They were also used to power machinery in mines. Score a point if you got any of these.

A steamship made in 1850.

★ 7. a) The period of change following the invention of the steam engine is called the Industrial Revolution.
8. Cinema came before television. The first cinema showing was made in Paris in 1895, by Auguste and Louis Lumière.
9. b) The first regular TV broadcasts were made in 1936. The first color broadcast was in 1953.
10. b) Inoculations are also called vaccinations. This comes from the Latin word *vacca*, meaning "cow."
11. True. Dairymaids often caught cowpox from the cows they milked. Jenner noticed that those who had caught cowpox rarely got smallpox.
12. c) A cold cannot be prevented by inoculation. Here are some more diseases, though, that can: polio, chicken pox, whooping cough, typhoid and cholera.
13. b) Darwin's theory was called evolution (see page 51).
14. a) The birds are all types of finch.
★ 15. The correct order of invention is: b) steam power, c) electricity, a) nuclear power. The first steam engine was made in about 1700. Electric power was first produced by a battery made in 1800. Nuclear power was first demonstrated in 1942.

The first electric battery looked like this.

The Wild West

★ 1. The Indian tent on page 52 is a tepee. Score a point if you said tepee or wigwam, though, as many Indians lived in wigwams. A wigwam (shown below) was often covered with leaves and branches.

Wigwam

2. The tents were made from buffalo hides. Score a point if you said leather or animal skins.

★ 3. An American Indian woman is called a squaw.

4. b) For good luck in battle, Indians danced a wardance.

5. c) American Indians wore moccasins on their feet.

6. c) The cattle are longhorn cattle.

7. True. Horses were taken to America by Spanish conquerors about 500 years ago. American Indians tamed and rode the horses that escaped from the Spaniards.

★ 8. It is a lasso or lariat. This is a rope with a loop tied with a sliding knot.

If the loop is tugged, the knot tightens. **Sliding knot**

9. a) The Indians called guns "smoke sticks."

★10. c) They are all members of American Indian tribes except a Zulu, who is a South African tribesperson.

★11. Canada and the USA make up North America. Score a point if you got them both. The other countries are in South America.

Alaska is part of the USA. **Canada** **USA** **NORTH AMERICA**

12. a) Most cowboys wore stetsons.

13. Cowboys' hats had wide brims to keep the sun out of their eyes.

14. The pistol was called a six-shooter because it fired six shots before it had to be reloaded.

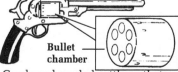

Bullet chamber

★15. Cowboys branded cattle so that they knew who the cattle belonged to. If branded cattle were stolen, people could identify them.

Trains, cars and planes

1. There are seven different forms of transportation on pages 54-55: horse and carriage, train, horseback, car, balloon, plane and airship. Only score a point if you spotted all seven.

2. True. A galloping horse can travel at 28mph (45kmph). The first trains went at about 12mph (20kmph).

3. No. The Russian Empire collapsed in 1923 (see page 54).

★ 4. b) The longest railway is the Trans-Siberian Railway. The area it crosses (shown on the map on page 54) is called Siberia.

★ 5. A modern car company that uses Karl Benz's name is Mercedes-Benz. A car made by Mercedes-Benz has this badge.

6. The handle, called a crank, was turned to start the engine. The first car that had a starter motor was made by Cadillac in 1912.

1912 Cadillac

7. b) For several years the Ford Model T was only available in black. For speed, Ford used quick-drying paint, which, until 1923, was only made in black.

★ 8. The car is a Beetle, or Bug.

★ 9. The engine of a Volkswagen Beetle is at the back of the car.

10. a) Air-filled tires are called pneumatic tires. The word comes from the Greek word *pneuma*, meaning "breath."

11. a) Volkswagen means "people's car" in German.

12. a) The canoe came first. This was probably the earliest form of transport. The bicycle was invented in 1839.

13. False. However, the earliest designs for aircraft, such as those by Leonardo da Vinci (1452-1519), included flapping wings.

Leonardo da Vinci's design for a man-powered aircraft.

14.

15. False. Although Zeppelins were huge, most of the space was filled with gas. Passengers sat in the gondola (see picture on page 55). Even large Zeppelins could carry only 50 or so people.

The twentieth century

1. The Bolshevik flag was red. You can see one in the first picture on page 56. The communist government later put a hammer and sickle on the flag. These represented the tools used by industrial workers and rural peasants.

2. True. Nicholas II was the last tsar.

★ 3. The Nazi leader was Adolf Hitler. He became *Führer* (leader) of Germany in 1933. He killed himself in 1945 when the Nazis lost World War II.

★ 4. b) The Nazi symbol was a swastika.

Swastika

5. No. The German army did not invade Great Britain.

6. b) Countries that join forces are called allies.

7. World War II lasted six years, from 1939-1945. More than 50 million people died during it. That is about as many people as live in Australia, Canada and Holland put together.

8. a) There have been two World Wars. World War I lasted from 1914-1918.

9. b) A war between people of the same country is called a civil war.

★10. The USSR was the first country to have a communist government. Score a point if you guessed USSR, Russia or the Russian Empire.

11. c) It is called a chip.

12. False. Silicon Valley has this name because so much computer industry is based there.

★13. The first people on the moon came from the USA. Between 1969 and 1972, six US missions explored the moon. The last two took vehicles, called lunar rovers, with them. The lunar rovers are still on the moon.

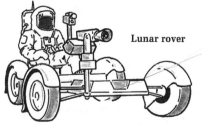

Lunar rover

★14. b) Argentina is a country in South America. Nigeria is in west Africa and Kenya is in east Africa.

15. Algeria was ruled by France before it won independence in 1962.

History Megaquiz answers

There are 100 possible points in the History Megaquiz. If you score over 50 you have done well. Over 75 is an excellent score. You can find out more about each answer on the page listed after it.

Famous people

1. j) Charles Darwin (page 51).
2. f) Tutankhamen (page 37).
3. h) Saladin (page 45).
4. g) Great Speaker (page 48).
5. i) Karl Benz (page 54).
6. b) Orville Wright (page 55).
7. a) Adolf Hitler (page 56).
8. c) Galileo (page 50).
9. e) Nicholas II (page 56).
10. d) Odysseus (pages 38 and 39).

Clothes and fashion

1. Anubis or Egyptian priest (page 36).
2. Crusader (pages 44 and 45).
3. Amelia Bloomer (page 50).
4. Aztec (page 49).
5. Cowboy (pages 52 and 53).
6. Roman (pages 40 and 41).
7. American Indian (page 52).
8. Egyptian (page 36).
9. Greek or Spartan soldier (page 39).
10. Viking (pages 42 and 43).

True or false?

1. False (page 40).
2. True (page 43).
3. False (page 52).
4. False (page 57).
5. True (page 38).
6. True (page 51).
7. False (page 55).
8. False (page 47).
9. True (page 48).
10. False (page 39).

Which came first?

1. Jellyfish; Stegosaurus; T. rex.
2. Viking; *conquistador*; Bolshevik.
3. Horse and cart; steam engine; computer.
4. Sword; cannon; six-shooter.
5. Tutankhamen; Richard I; Nicholas II.
6. Water well; inoculation; television.
7. Chariot; Viking longship; Model T Ford.
8. Pyramid; Palace of Alhambra; nuclear power station.
9. Homer; Amelia Bloomer; Lenin.
10. Roman Empire; Inca Empire; USSR.

Close-ups

1. Tomahawk (page 52).
2. Greek actor's mask (page 38).
3. Castle (page 46).
4. Tutankhamen's mask (page 37).
5. Tyrannosaurus rex (page 35).
6. Aztec Great Temple (page 49).
7. Mirror (page 45).
8. Computer chip (page 57).
9. Viking longship (page 43).
10. Early television (page 50).

Where in the world?

1. India (page 53).
2. China (page 57).
3. Chernobyl (page 51).
4. Spain (page 49).
5. Egypt (page 37).
6. Mexico (page 48).
7. Olympia (page 39).
8. Rome (page 41).
9. Italy (page 50).
10. England (page 54).

The time line

1. About 40,000 years ago (page 35).
2. About 800BC (page 38).
3. 1521 (page 49).
4. 100 million years ago (page 34).
5. About 2,630BC (pages 36 and 37).
6. 0AD (page 40).
7. About 750AD (pages 42 and 43).
8. 1096 (page 44).
9. About 1400 (page 47).
10. 1969 (page 57).

What do you know?

1. In the sand (page 37).
2. Dinosaurs (page 34).
3. Women or slaves. Score a point for either (page 38).
4. Bards (page 43).
5. Volkswagen (page 55).
6. Emperor (page 56).
7. The gun (page 49).
8. Black-and-white (page 50).
9. A castle (page 46).
10. Animal skins (page 52).

Silhouettes

1. Dinosaur or Parasaurolophus (page 35).
2. Power station (page 51).
3. Greek athlete (page 39).
4. Tepee or wigwam (page 52).
5. Benz's car or early car (page 54).
6. Finch or bird (page 51).
7. Mangonel (page 47).
8. Roman chariot (page 41).
9. Pyramids (pages 36 and 37).
10. Invicta or steam engine (page 54).

What else do you know?

1. Brachiosaurus (page 34).
2. USSR (page 57).
3. Tragedies (page 38).
4. Hot air (page 55).
5. One day (page 48).
6. Fights, or the Games (pages 40 and 41).
7. Nuclear fuel (page 51).
8. Yes (page 40).
9. Richard I or "the Lionheart" (page 45).
10. Ranches (page 52).

Index

The photos on page 56 are reproduced by kind permission of the Imperial War Museum, London. The cartoon on page 51 is reproduced by kind permission of the Trustees of the British Museum. The Mercedes-Benz badge on page 63 is reproduced by kind permission of Mercedes Benz AG, Stuttgart, Germany.